Ms. Marshall has written a riveting book that details her travails adopting two children. Social Services' numerous omissions of information, changes of biological parents rights, and failure to support the adoptive family's needs set the stage for a scary story that reads like fiction but, unfortunately, is not.

As a Licensed Marriage and Family Therapist specializing in adoption, I believe Ms. Marshall's book is unique but, unfortunately, the story of her adoption experience is not. The country's adoption policy is broken, wreaking havoc on many adoptive families. Kudos to Ms. Marshall for her relentless determination to defend her new family.

—*June Mikkelsen, licensed marriage and family therapist specializing in adoption*

Catherine Marshall's openhearted and honest account of foster parent adoption is the first authentic report of the truth behind our broken foster care system, which fails young children most in need of parenting. Catherine tells her own story of the doubts, risks, and hopes that go into adoption of troubled foster children, and the morning-after realization of taking on so much more than she ever imagined. Her fair-minded report of her fight for her children's future somehow comforts my wife, Annie, and me in our frustration and grief at this system that stripped our foster daughter of her best chance for a good life.

—*Bill Baker, former foster parent*

I was captivated by Catherine's story. It should be required reading for all prospective parents of foster kids. My own experience was similar. I expected that giving a child a loving, stable environment would ensure she would become a happy adult. Not so. It's much more complicated than that.

—*Alice Bonner, former foster parent*

The Easter Moose

THE EASTER MOOSE

ONE FAMILY'S JOURNEY ADOPTING THROUGH FOSTER CARE

Catherine Marshall

CAPBUILDERS PUBLISHING

The names of most of those mentioned in this book have been changed.

Design by Meadowlark Publishing Services.

Illustrations on pp. iv and 100 by the author.
Cover illustration: ©iStockphoto.com/artist: Floortje

Published by Capbuilders Publishing.
www.catmarshall.net

Manufactured in the United States of America.
ISBN 978-0-9850561-2-4
Published 2015

For my children

Contents

Contents

PREFACE

The Easter Moose is not a how-to manual for those thinking about adopting children through foster care. Nor is it a cautionary tale. Many of the troublesome conditions plaguing foster adoption in the late 1980s and early 1990s were remedied by regulations. It is not a vendetta against social services. While there were difficulties with certain social workers and the court system, the county agency provided the necessary financial support for the children's special needs. This story is also not a demonstration of therapeutic parenting. Little was known about attachment disorder at that time and mistakes were made.

I wrote *The Easter Moose* to tell a story that is rarely told. When I shared my experiences with other foster and adoptive parents, I was touched by how they had similar experiences and were haunted by feelings of frustration, loss and failure. Many foster and adoptive parents continue to suffer with guilt because their efforts did not result in happy-ever-after endings.

Like many foster-adopt parents of older children, I first believed nurture would triumph over nature. Adoption and foster care memoirs tend to reinforce that notion. Many popular books focus on the stories of successful adults who, by their own will and determination, overcame horrifying foster care experiences. There are also a few wonderful accounts of foster or adoptive parents navigating the hurdles of foreign adoption or raising children with special needs. While these memoirs are inspiring, I believe a different, more common experience is worth sharing.

The last thing I want is to discourage foster adoption. In the U.S., over 107,000 foster children are ready for adoption. Foster-adoption continues to be relatively low cost compared to adopting internationally and many foster adoption agencies provide financial support. At the end of this book there is a list of foster care and adoption resources you might find useful.

I hope it doesn't spoil anything to say there is no tidy ending to my memoir. My children are now raising their own children and facing the trials of daily life, shadowed by their childhood experiences. They have accomplished a lot, in spite of their rough start. They are my heroes and someday they may tell their own stories. Their names have been changed in this memoir to protect their privacy.

Finally, I hope this story provides the reader with a better understanding of the experience of some foster parents. Some of you may find comfort, and maybe a dose of forgiveness and acceptance. *The Easter Moose* is for all parents who feel they have failed their children. In the end, we may never know the full affect our parenting had, and, at some point we must say to ourselves, we did the best we could.

ACKNOWLEDGMENTS

I am deeply grateful for the support of my fellow writers of Mendocino including my teacher, Norma Watkins, who demonstrated what creative nonfiction is all about, the volunteers who run the annual Mendocino Coast Writers Conference and the members of my writers' group, Bill Baker, Orah Young, Michela Conti, Willow Hay-Arthur, Gloria Schoofs Jorgensen and Sue Gibson. Without these folks prodding and encouraging, I would have given up. I thank my partner and soulmate, "Steve," who supported this writing with his infinite patience. My friends and editors, Sheridan and Stan of Meadowlark Publishing Services, have done it again with their professionalism and grace. I appreciate and continue to be in awe of my children who beat the odds and now thrive with families of their own.

1

THE SIBLING GROUP

I studied the Polaroid in my hand. The little girl wore a cornflower blue sun dress and white sandals, and her short, baby-fine blond hair framed her chubby face. She grinned as if someone had coached her to say cheese. I knew she was three, but her wide blue eyes and baby fat made her look younger. She sat on an ottoman and a little boy stood beside her, his hand firmly on her shoulder like he was trying to make sure she stayed put. He wore an orange matching shorts-and-shirt outfit that looked like something a little girl would wear. His hair was light brown, parted and plastered down. Though he was six, he was small and thin and bore the serious expression of someone with a lot on his mind.

I handed the photo to my husband, Michael. The social worker in charge of foster placement, Louise, sat across from us in our family room. She looked like she'd dressed in a hurry: rumpled clothes and tangled hair. A photo album containing pictures of other children available for adoption lay next to her on the loveseat. We all ignored the buzzing of the pager in the large purse at her feet.

"Why do you think we would be a good match for these two?" Michael asked. I wondered about this as well. To be considered for the Department of Social Services Foster-Adopt program, we had completed an extensive application listing our education, job experience, hobbies, and the languages we spoke. The agency had rejected our earlier application to adopt a baby because Michael, at forty-three, was considered too old. Something must have been right for DSS to believe we were eligible to adopt what they called a "sibling group" of older children.

Louise looked down at the clipboard in her lap, searching for clues. "Well, you live in Livermore. There are good schools here, and both the kids may need special education." She nodded and smiled at us. "I also thought because you were an older couple, you might be interested in getting a family right away, in one fell swoop, so to speak."

Michael squinted at the photo and, perplexed, looked up at Louise. "About that," he said. "Why would we qualify for a toddler but not a baby?"

I'd hoped Michael wouldn't bring that up. I didn't think this woman had any control over such decisions.

"I'm sorry. The Foster-Adopt program has different criteria, mostly because the children have been in foster care for a while, for various reasons. I'm afraid newborns are in big demand and there's a long waiting list of approved foster parents." She continued undaunted. "There are some complications with Robert and Jenny, but I don't think they're too inconvenient."

Robert and Jenny had an older brother, Timmy, who wasn't up for adoption. He lived at a separate foster home because he had behavior problems and was aggressive with the younger two. The three children had been placed in foster care when the police responded to a domestic violence complaint and saw their living conditions. Drug paraphernalia, garbage, dirty clothes, and broken glass were strewn about the one room they lived in, and the children were showing signs of neglect. The parents had been given more than two years to improve their situation and get their children back. When it was clear they weren't making any progress toward meeting the requirements, the courts ordered adoption for Jenny and Robert.

"We think it best the children retain some supervised contact with their brother," Louise continued. "If you were to foster these children, you'd need to help with that."

"Are the parents out of the picture? What's to prevent them from showing up and interfering with the adoption?" I asked. Michael handed the photo back to Louise.

She smiled and leaned forward.

"We've anticipated this. Your name and address will be kept secret— you won't come in contact with them. You'll have the support of DSS throughout the process. The courts have ordered adoption for these children. All we need is a nice couple like you to give them a good home."

Michael and I looked at each other, both worried about the same thing. Taking the kids to visit their brother once in a while was reasonable, but the birth parents might be trouble. It was important to us that we not have to deal with them. I was a little frightened by the prospect of having these people show up at our doorstep demanding their kids back. We had enrolled in the Foster-Adopt program for the sole purpose of adopting, not haggling with birth parents about custody.

Louise handed back the photo. "Keep this. I think you'll feel better once you've met the children. Shall I set up an appointment for you?"

2

A Balancing Act

Our new place in Livermore needed work. We'd been living in a brand new condo nearby: perfect for a couple, but not a family. We had sold it for a dark red, ranch-style, single-story home—an anomaly in this neighborhood of more neutrally painted models. The harvest gold kitchen appliances had seen better days and the green shag carpet was worn and ripped. On the plus side, the interior had an inviting, open layout and the backyard was large enough for a vegetable garden. The neighborhood was quiet and safe, with a large park nearby, and the family room had a view of the hills and windmills of Altamont Pass.

The biggest drawback was that it had no air conditioning, unthinkable in the hot Livermore Valley. When we bought it we'd thought we could postpone installing AC by just using fans and letting the breeze blow through the open windows. But by July, temperatures exceeded 110 degrees and the only breeze was a dust-laden wind that left us parched and cranky. In the evening, the outside temperature cooled down but the house did not. After a few sweaty nights, I called some contractors for quotes. This unplanned expense, on top of the larger mortgage, was causing additional strain on our finances. Michael and I squabbled about money, his daughter's impending visit, and the possibility of adopting two children.

When we had been turned down for a baby adoption, we invited Michael's teenage daughter to come live with us for her senior year of high school. Kayla lived with her mother, her stepdad, and stepsisters in

Toronto. It was shortly after we made those plans for Kayla to move in that we got the call about the two foster children.

"Kayla was looking forward to having us all to herself for her senior year. I don't think she'll be happy sharing us with two foster kids," Michael said.

"Kayla's a sweetie. She knew we were considering adopting. She'll understand," I said.

"What about furniture and clothes?"

"Louise said DSS gives stipends for new clothes, and used furniture isn't that much. A couple of beds and a dresser from St. Vincent de Paul will cost next to nothing." I wasn't thrilled about being the cheerleader, but one of us needed to see the bright side. After a year of trying to conceive, the decision to explore adoption through foster care was one we'd made together. I didn't like having to twist his arm now, and wished he'd be as excited as I was about meeting the two little ones.

Robert and Jenny were staying in an emergency foster home not far from us. I was surprised to learn that these licensed shelters operated in residential neighborhoods as places to quickly house children when they were removed from dangerous situations. I knew that in Jenny and Robert's case, their previous foster parents had requested the children's removal after an unpleasant encounter with the birth parents. So when Louise called to set up the first meeting with the children, I asked again whether we would have to deal with them.

"Mrs. Sievert, we've been over this. The children's location and your identity will be kept secret. I really don't see this as anything you have to worry about." She didn't seem to be taking my concerns seriously, and before I could ask more questions, she changed the subject.

"The appointment is set for this Saturday afternoon. Robert and Jenny are aware that you're considering becoming their foster parents, but we've made no promises. We haven't talked to them about adoption yet. I really don't think they would even understand what that means at this point." She gave me the address and phone number of the emergency foster home and said good-bye as her pager sounded in the background.

When I conveyed the conversation to Michael, he was not reassured. "It's bad enough we have to be under the supervision of DSS as foster parents—if we have birth parents to deal with, this will be intolerable."

During the informational meeting about the Foster Adopt program, we had learned that if we wanted to adopt a child we first needed to become certified as foster parents. This meant taking classes on parenting and first aid, having our home inspected, and undergoing background checks and medical exams. Though we were entitled to receive a small monthly stipend to help with the children's expenses, we were subject to oversight by the agency. I chafed at the condescending tone of the department's many memos and directives, which seemed to imply we must be innately reckless and stupid. These precautions were understandable, but for us, becoming foster parents was a means to an end. Some of the others in our classes were looking at foster care as a job, but we had no intention of making a career out of this. If we were to adopt children through this program, our plan would be to get in, adopt the kids, and get out of the system as quickly as possible.

"If they keep our address and phone number secret as DSS promised," I told Michael, "we should be okay. Let's see how we feel about the kids and then go from there."

When we pulled up in front of the emergency foster home, I was struck by how unremarkable it looked. The front lawn was mowed and edged, and box shrubs lined the front walk. The beige stucco was the same as every other house on the block, distinguished only by blue trim and a hanging flower basket at the front door. I wondered if the neighbors were accustomed to police officers dropping off children at all hours.

The woman who answered the door was short and thin and wore a crisp shirtdress and flats. Her medium-length brown hair was held back with a plastic headband, and she wore a small gold cross around her neck. Her smile was pleasant, but looked as if she'd lost sleep. She introduced herself as Sharon and shook Michael's hand. A baby whimpered from a bassinet in the hall.

"Crack baby," she said, pointing with her chin at the bassinet as she took my hand. "Poor thing's going through withdrawal. I've been up all night.

"Jenny, Robert, your visitors are here," she called up the stairs, her voice a loud whisper so as not to startle the infant.

Robert came down first, followed by Jenny, who grabbed the bannister with both hands, navigating each step with her chubby legs. Robert wore a pair of pull-up jeans and an orange tank top with a cartoon character on the front. His face was solemn as we introduced ourselves. Jenny wore a pink sundress with a matching hair bow and a pair of white sandals. She looked excited about the prospect of meeting us, or perhaps going for an outing.

"Why don't you take them across the street to the park to get acquainted?" Sharon suggested.

I tried a perky tone, like a school teacher. "Great idea. Is that okay with you two?"

Robert said, "Sure, that's okay. We go there all the time. I'll show you." He led the way, trudging on like a little soldier. I took Jenny's hand as she looked up and offered a charming smile.

I said, "That's a very pretty dress, Jenny."

"She doesn't know how to talk yet," Robert said.

Michael took charge at the crosswalk. "Let's hold hands when we cross the street." He made a show of looking both ways. We arrived at a swing set, and Michael asked if they wanted a push. Robert sat down on the big-kid swings and proceeded to push himself, not waiting for Michael to get him started. Jenny raised her arms, signaling that she wanted me to pick her up and place her in the baby swings. As I did, I noticed her bulky diapers. I thought about the neglect that had resulted in a three-and-a-half-year-old still not toilet trained. I knew I could fix this if she were mine.

I glanced over at Michael and Robert and saw them talking while Michael pushed the swing.

I bent over to speak to Jenny. "Would you like to play on the jungle gym?" She looked at me and smiled, her expression reminding me of the agreeable look foreigners adopt when they have no idea what you're saying but don't want to hurt your feelings. I led her over to the metal jungle gym, lifted her onto a low bar, and held her till she could get her bearings. I realized too late that her flat-soled sandals weren't suitable for this kind of play. She slipped off the bars and didn't hold on to balance herself. I lifted her off and set her on the ground. Jenny needed proper clothes and a pair of tennis shoes so she could have more freedom to run and play—but I was getting ahead of myself. Michael and I needed to talk, and he might not feel the same way. We played with the children for about twenty minutes, then headed back to the foster home.

"Are you going to be our parents?" Robert asked.

Michael's back was to me as we walked along the sidewalk; I had no way to gauge his reaction to this question.

"I don't know, Robert." I said. "We'll have to see."

3

MAKING A LIST

The following week, Michael and I spent our evenings grappling with the decision of whether to adopt Jenny and Robert, considering what we knew and calculating the adjustments we'd have to make to our home and our lives.

"What do we know about these kids?" Michael asked. "Jenny's definitely delayed, but I think it's because they've been in too many foster homes, seven now counting the emergency one. Maybe she'll catch up once we get her into preschool."

"That's what I think. Can you believe she's still in diapers?" I was glad Michael was seeing the possibilities.

"Robert is so serious. He's like a little old man in kid's clothes. Smart, though." Michael seemed intent on convincing himself, and I didn't want to interfere.

"I think he's been parenting Jenny for a while. The little guy needs to have a chance to be a kid," I said. Letting Michael work this through on his own was a strategy I'd learned early in our relationship. If he thought I was arguing, I'd get nowhere.

"We can't do this without the kids in day care and school. We both have to work full time to afford this," he said. Michael was an artist and ran an art gallery in Hayward, and I worked in computer sales for a startup in Manteca. Our mortgage and other bills didn't leave much wiggle room.

"I think our being organized is what makes this so doable. We should be able to manage things, especially with Kayla here," I said. I knew as soon as I said it that it didn't sound right. We didn't want Kayla to feel like we were taking advantage of her.

"But we agreed we want her to enjoy her senior year, right?"

"Yes, that's true," I said. We would have to juggle things so none of the children felt slighted. We were both quiet as Michael opened a bottle of wine.

Then it hit him at the same time it occurred to me. "If we decide to do this, we're going to go from being childless to having three children—practically overnight." I nodded and took a sip from my wine glass. Our house had been very quiet, too quiet for me. It would be fun to fill the silence with the energetic chaos of children.

We let Louise know the first outing had gone well, and she encouraged us to make another appointment to spend more time with the kids. She seemed anxious to move the process along. The emergency foster home would only be available for a couple more weeks, so if we didn't proceed with the adoption, the kids would have to be placed into yet another regular foster care setting elsewhere.

We scheduled our next outing with the children for the following Saturday afternoon at Del Valle Reservoir, a local recreation spot with picnicking and swimming. Robert and Jenny were relaxed and playful and didn't show any nervousness about spending an afternoon with us. I wondered if their multiple foster placements had helped them become more adaptable to new situations.

Jenny was so fair skinned we made sure she wore a floppy hat. We lathered both kids with sunblock and tried to stay in the shade, where we played in the sand with beach toys we'd picked up at the supermarket. All afternoon Jenny pointed and smiled if she wanted something. Once in a while she spoke baby talk, saying words like *wa wa* for water when she was thirsty. Robert played interpreter, told us what kind of food Jenny liked, and warned us she could be a problem.

"If you give her any vegetables, she holds 'em in her cheeks and spits 'em out when you're not looking," he said. "And if you give her too much candy, she gets sick. Once she pooped all day long because she got into my Halloween candy."

Michael and I exchanged knowing looks. It was going to be a challenge to get Robert to relax and let us be the parents.

"We'll try to remember that," I said. "It's nice you're looking out for your little sister."

"Well, she minds me. If you have any trouble with her, just let me know."

By the end of the day we were all very wet, dirty, and tired. I did my best to clean up the kids before taking them back and apologized to Sharon for the sand. She waved away my concern and asked the kids if they'd had a good time. As she closed the door, I heard her directing them to scoot up the stairs for a shower. On the way back to the car, I realized how intensely I wanted to be the one to feed them, give them a bath, and tell them a bedtime story.

The next day we got a call from Louise, who wanted to know whether we would be deciding soon about fostering the kids. She reminded us that the school year was starting and both of them needed to be registered, Robert for first grade and Jenny for a special education preschool. Robert could attend the elementary school across the street from our home and his after-school day care was located on the same campus near his classroom. Louise had located a special ed preschool a few miles away. They had an opening for Jenny, but we'd have to contact the teachers to conduct an assessment and develop what was called an "Individual Education Plan (IEP)" for her. We needed to buy bedroom furniture, find day care for Jenny, and complete our foster care licensing requirements. There was a lot of pressure to make a decision—and a giant to-do list to act on if we said yes.

Every time Louise called, I took notes about deadlines, contact names, and acronyms we'd have to learn. I felt competent organizing these details, but I wasn't sure if Michael had the patience for all of this. If he felt overwhelmed or pressured, he might say no to everything. I decided I might as well lay it all out and find out where he stood. It was decision time.

"Louise filled me in on the school deadlines. If we proceed, she needs us to move the kids in by the end of next week—otherwise she has to take them to another foster home. Are we ready to do this?"

Michael was deep in thought, staring through the glass patio doors toward our weedy back yard.

"All right, then." He nodded as he continued looking off in the distance. "We can do this." I was surprised and relieved—we did agree on some things. Michael and I were both the oldest in our families and had learned responsibility at a young age. We knew we were capable enough, and we knew these children needed us. Our competence and their need were a good match. It seemed like it was meant to be.

"I'll give her a call tomorrow," I said. We were starting a family.

❖

Years later, looking back on this decision, I often wondered, *What were we thinking?* With the little information we had to go on, how could we have made the commitment to take on the care of these two children? If we'd known what lay ahead, I'm not sure we would ever have agreed.

When I called Louise back to let her know Michael and I were ready to move ahead, I again sought reassurance that we wouldn't have to deal with the birth parents interfering when it came time for adoption. Louise reminded me she had court papers from the previous November ordering a permanent plan of adoption for the children, but at that time there had been no foster-adopt parents available. She mentioned that another court hearing was scheduled in a couple of weeks with the birth father; he and his attorney were alleging the county had not given him enough support in his effort at family reunification while he was in jail. She was certain the judge would dismiss his claims and the adoption could proceed. She then changed the subject to finalizing the details of our foster care licensing.

When I got off the phone, I went to my desk in our bedroom and pulled out a new spiral notebook and a sharpened pencil. It would be easy to become overwhelmed with all the details stemming from our decision to move ahead, so I made a checklist of what we needed to do. I also marked the date of the new hearing on my calendar and made a note to follow up to learn the result.

4

TIDY AND ORGANIZED

Kayla had second thoughts about joining us with the children coming at the same time, but she figured she couldn't change her mind—she'd already told all of her friends she was moving to California. Her mother was also anxious for her to make the trip, looking forward to a break from the frequent mother and daughter dramas. Kayla arrived the following week, tired from the long flight and resigned to the prospect of sharing space with the two children.

She was a tall, slender teen with dark hair and eyes. She slouched when she sat and often covered her face with her hand if anyone tried to take her picture or give her a compliment. Like most seventeen-year-old girls, she was self-conscious and critical of her appearance. She had a pretty smile and clear skin, but she thought her nose was too long and her chin too pointy.

Kayla had a dramatic flair and was artistic like her father. She loved to draw and paint and, when she thought no one was looking, twirl around the room like a ballerina, lost in the music coming from her Walkman. During her previous visits, Kayla and I had become friends. She confided in me about her problems with her mother and stepfather, and she cheered me up when Michael sank into one of his dark moods. I found her to be delightful company and was happy to have her join us.

Kayla settled into her bedroom, unpacking her bags and arranging pictures on her dresser. I noticed her jeans were worn and her blouse didn't fit well. Though Michael had provided child support to his ex-wife over the years, it was clear little of that money had gone to Kayla's wardrobe. She was going to need school clothes, and I hoped she didn't have expensive tastes. I thought we could probably get away with buying the younger children secondhand clothes, but that wasn't going to work for a teenage girl. We went shopping at Kmart, using a credit card that was dangerously close to the limit. While we browsed I talked with Kayla about Robert and Jenny moving in.

"You're a dear for being so understanding about Jenny and Robert. I think you'll like them. They're very sweet."

"It'll work out. I needed a break. I hate living at home right now. Mom yells at me all the time and spoils my little sisters. I'm looking forward to spending some special time with you and Dad."

"We'll work on that," I replied. I made a vow to myself to carve out time for Kayla. It would be easy for her to get lost in the confusion, and this year was a special time for her.

"Sure," Kayla said. Looking distracted by the choice of shoes before her, she asked, "Are you having any more problems with Dad?"

Her question caught me off guard. We had never talked about her visit last summer when Michael lost his temper and slapped me during our vacation to Los Angeles. I had to wear dark glasses for half the trip.

"He has his moods, but no more hitting. We went to counseling and I think he's got it under control." She continued to look occupied with her shopping.

"Don't worry. I'm fine," I said.

After that incident, Kayla had confided in me that she'd once seen Michael hit her mother, and she worried her dad and me were going to divorce too. Since we'd married two years ago, there'd been other incidents that prompted couples therapy sessions and second thoughts on my part. I was on guard for Michael's dark moods but figured as long as he went to therapy and the stress level stayed down, we'd be fine.

The children were scheduled to join us in three days. Meanwhile, we had a few more details to settle. We'd discussed sleeping arrangements with the social worker and she seemed fine with Robert and Jenny sharing a bedroom, at least for a little while. This gave Kayla a chance to have her own room for now. We arranged the little ones' room with two twin beds and a nightstand and lamp in between. There was still a chance Jenny could fall out of bed so we installed a bed rail for her. We cheered up the room with bright bedspreads and sheets, a sports theme for Robert, and Disney characters for Jenny. Each child had a chest of drawers and a section of the closet for shoes and toys. Though the kids already had bags of toys, I splurged on a couple more: a set of Legos for Robert and a musical keyboard with the ABCs for Jenny. I placed the toys on their beds as welcome gifts.

I surveyed their bedroom one last time before we set out to bring them home. Everything was tidy and organized. I didn't expect the room to stay that way, but it was very satisfying to see it laid out in preparation. Kayla was getting settled and the kids would be there soon.

As we drove to the emergency foster home to pick up the kids, I recalled the time Michael and I went camping together a couple of years before. After arriving at the campsite we set up the tent, unrolled our sleeping bags, cracked open a bottle of wine, and settled into our lawn chairs for an afternoon of quiet reading. The silence that bore down on us prompted a discussion of how "tidy and organized" our lives were and how that couldn't be all there was for us. We joked that we needed a little chaos in our lives, and now our dream of filling our home with a family was about to come true.

5

THEN THERE WERE FIVE

When we arrived at the foster home, the children were inside waiting on the stairs, packed and ready to go. Two duffle bags were piled in the foyer along with a garbage bag stuffed with their toys. Sharon, their foster mother for the past two weeks, hugged the kids and planted a kiss on Jenny's cheek.

"You two be good," she said.

"Bye-bye, Mom," Jenny said. I smiled at Sharon but raised my eyebrows. I knew emergency foster homes took care not to confuse the kids.

"She calls every woman Mom," she said. I was shocked that my new little daughter had been shunted to so many homes the word had lost all meaning.

Jenny turned to me with the same engaging smile she had flashed when we met and took my hand. With my free arm, I hugged the woman who'd been so kind to us, then threw one of the kid's duffle bags over my shoulder. Michael scooped up the rest of the pile and Robert rushed out the door, bent on retrieving his bicycle from the driveway.

It took a moment to figure out where to stow everything in our little Honda. With the bicycle in the trunk there wasn't much room for the rest of the kids' stuff. After we got the children situated in the backseat, we stuffed bags between them and on the floor. I struggled with the mechanics of Jenny's car seat straps and Robert insisted on showing us he was old enough to work the seat belt himself. I balanced a bag on my lap while Michael drove our packed car the short distance home.

"Kayla is looking forward to meeting you both." I told the kids. "She's a lot of fun. Robert, did you know we live right across the street from your school?"

"You know I'm supposed to be in first grade, right?" he said.

"We know that, Robert. You don't have to worry. We took care of everything."

He nodded and frowned as he looked out the window, evidently not entirely convinced.

Robert's concerns were not unfounded. What with the mad dash of getting certified for foster care, furnishing two bedrooms, and registering all three kids for school, perfection was nowhere to be found. Even with both of us taking time off from work, we felt overwhelmed and unprepared.

We were also worried about Kayla and the kids getting along. In a perfect world the children would all have gotten to know one another before they moved in together. But when we arrived at the house, I was relieved to see that Kayla went out of her way to make the kids feel at home, showing them their room and helping them unpack. She even gave them a little tour of the house and explained where to find the towels and put their toothbrushes. Following along with Kayla's tour, I pointed out the little potty next to the toilet.

"See, Jenny, that's just for you. Do you have to go potty?"

Jenny smiled agreeably and let me tug off her diaper for a trial run. I closed the toilet lid and took a seat to keep her company.

"What a big girl you are," I said. She smiled. I smiled. The moments passed. I made a mental note to bring children's books into the bathroom to keep us busy. After about ten minutes of smiling and encouragement and hearing no indication of success, I helped her off the potty and snapped on another diaper. I lifted her onto a toddler stool so she could wash her hands. No use trying to pressure her now.

While Jenny and I were occupied in the bathroom, Michael, Kayla, and Robert explored the backyard. The afternoon gusts had picked up, but the temperature remained in the nineties and dust swirled about the yard. Jenny and I watched them from the patio door. We had fans blowing throughout the house and window shades pulled closed to keep out the beating sun. The air conditioning unit would be installed next week, thanks to the contractor's convenient payment plan.

"Come on inside, everybody." I said. "We can make lemonade. Kayla, why don't you show them their new toys?"

She brought out the welcome gifts and set them on the family room rug in front of the fan. I opened up the Lego set and dumped the pieces onto the floor, hoping to interest Robert in constructing something. Michael and Kayla went to the kitchen to mix up the lemonade while I wrestled Jenny's musical ABC toy out of its protective plastic. I lifted Jenny next to me on the loveseat, set the toy in her lap, and showed her how to punch the buttons to make sounds. While she banged away, Robert stared at the Lego pieces but made no move to assemble anything. Jenny found the button for "Mary Had a Little Lamb" and played it over and over until Robert put his hands over his ears.

Michael served everyone their drinks and then plopped into the sofa across from me. Kayla surveyed the scene and opted for the peace and quiet of her bedroom, lemonade in hand.

Except for the fans, the room was quiet now because Jenny's hands were occupied with her lemonade cup. Both children peered at us as they sipped.

Michael sighed and studied the ceiling. "Shall we see what's on TV?"

6

Court Order

Our first week as a new family was as chaotic as could be expected when five people were learning to live together. But we were fortunate to have this time as a dry run for getting everyone out the door for school and work. I couldn't imagine how we were going to pull that off five days a week. For the time being, we convinced Kayla to put on her makeup in her bedroom while Michael and I helped the children get ready in the two bathrooms.

I made several attempts to get Jenny to use her new potty and we did have one success. I lavished her with praise, stopping short of fireworks and a press release, but it wasn't enough for her to break her dirty diaper habit.

Nighttime was a different routine of picking up toys, taking baths, and story time. Robert insisted he was old enough to take a shower by himself, but we learned his idea of bathing was dabbing at body parts with a dry washcloth. Michael helped him make sure he got everything clean.

After taking this first week to get the children settled, Michael went back to his job; Volunteers had run the art gallery in his absence. I had to get back to my work too, but I'd scheduled more time off to get the children settled in school and day care. Though my employer was a friend and a family man, and he understood why I needed this time, he'd sounded worried that I wouldn't come back.

There was much to do before the kids started school, and now I was on my own to get it done. Kayla stayed with Jenny while I walked Robert across the street to the elementary school. We met his teacher, who was busy prepping her classroom. Robert shook her hand like a grown-up and looked around the room while the teacher and I chatted. On the way back home he tried to impress me with what he already knew. "I can count to one hundred and I know how to read already."

"Really? Where did you learn all that?"

"I taught myself, from watching TV."

"Pretty impressive! First grade should be easy for you."

"Yeah, maybe I can help the teacher with the other kids."

Later, I gathered up all the children to start our errands. Kayla wanted me to drive by her high school first. We'd visited the campus once before, but she had to make sure she knew where to catch the city bus. The next stop was Jenny's day care. Janice, the owner, greeted us and asked her helper to show Jenny around and introduce her to the other kids. I explained that I needed help with her potty training so she could qualify for preschool, and Janice promised to help reinforce what we were trying at home. When we were ready to leave, Jenny lifted her arms to hug and kiss Janice good-bye. As we walked out the front door, she turned to Janice and waved. "Bye, Mom," she said. Janice gave me a look that said, *We'll work on that too.*

We dropped by the St. Vincent de Paul thrift store to look for school clothes for Robert and some play clothes for Jenny. I was determined to get something else for Jenny to wear besides those baby-doll sundresses. I found some pretty decent jeans and shirts for her, but I couldn't locate anything for six-year-old boys.

The cashier rolled her eyes when I asked about it. "Sugar, good used clothes for six-year-old boys do not exist. The job of little boys is to destroy things including clothes. Better hit the Kmart."

We all piled back into the car for more clothes shopping. Robert picked out a few T-shirts with action heroes on the front. He seemed embarrassed when I snuck a peek at the tag inside his pants to learn what size he wore.

A hair salon with a sign reading DROP-INS WELCOME was next on our list. Robert looked like he hadn't had a haircut in months; when his hair wasn't plastered down with water, overgrown cowlicks protruded at odd angles and bangs hung in his eyes. He made his preferences known to the barber, then fidgeted and scowled when hair fell on his face. As a reward for all our hard work we ordered cones at the Baskin-Robbins next door. Jenny smeared ice cream on her face and clothes while Robert ate without spilling a drop. I was touched when Kayla dipped her napkin into her water cup and mopped Jenny's face. She was such a good big sister and I was lucky to have her help.

When we arrived home in the late afternoon, I found several messages on our answering machine. One was the air conditioning contractor confirming tomorrow's work; another was the social worker Louise informing us that a visit with the children's brother was scheduled for the weekend. It would take place at their brother's foster home in Hayward on Sunday afternoon. *Why does this have to start just as we're getting the kids settled?* I tried not to look as perturbed as I felt.

Robert looked anxious when he heard the message. "Do we have to see Timmy?" His brow furrowed with concern.

"Don't you want to see your brother? I think it's been a few months since you got together."

"He beats me up. Next time, I'm going to practice my karate on him." He demonstrated his moves by flailing his arms through the air like a deranged Bruce Lee.

I knelt so we were eye to eye, hoping to reassure him. "Hold on, Robert. Nobody's going to beat you up. Michael and I will be there to make sure you don't get hurt." His chin dropped to his chest and his shoulders sagged. He had no confidence adults would take care of things.

"Let me see what I can do. Maybe we can just visit for a little while and then go home. We'll stay with you and make sure he doesn't hurt you." Robert shrugged me off and went to his room.

I called Louise back and got her voice mail. When she phoned an hour later she started off with an apology.

"You know, I really hate to do this to you after just a week. We got a call from the court and we have to comply. I'm sorry."

"You explained we have to take them to see their brother, so we're prepared for that," I said. "But I wish we could have waited until the kids were more settled."

"Well, the visit isn't just with the brother," she said. "They have to visit with their birth parents as well."

I sank onto the loveseat next to the phone.

"What do you mean? You promised we wouldn't have to deal with the parents. They were going to be kept out of the picture and we could start with the adoption." I was trying to keep my voice down so the children wouldn't hear.

"I'm sorry, Catherine. We didn't expect this. The birth father's attorney made a strong case to a new judge that the county hadn't given the father enough help while he was incarcerated. The judge ordered weekly visits starting this Sunday."

I was stunned. What I had worried about was coming to pass. "You have to do something, Louise! This is going to be so confusing to the kids. They'll think they're going back to their parents. ... They aren't—are they?" I couldn't believe this was happening. The beginning of a tension headache crept up my neck.

"You can drop the kids off at Timmy's foster home in the morning at ten a.m. and pick them up at four. The parents will be with the kids all day. Try not to be discouraged by this. Our department has the attorney on this and we plan to appeal the decision. We think the judge was not properly informed of the history."

If social services needed an attorney, where is this going? My heart sank.

"But we had plans to take the kids swimming this weekend, and we've invited friends over for a barbecue to meet them . . ." My voice trailed off, and I became aware of how helpless I sounded. Heat rose in my face.

"Look. This is not how you told us things would go." I was angry now and didn't care if I offended her or if anyone heard.

She responded in kind. "This is a court order, Mrs. Sievert. If you don't comply you will be held in contempt of court. Have the children there on Sunday. I'll call you next week to see how things went." Before I could protest further, she hung up.

I heard the front door slam. Michael was home early to help with dinner as he'd promised. I rose to greet him, pondering how I would break this distressing news. Jenny and Robert came running out of their room when they heard the door. Jenny rushed to Michael and hugged him around his knees. Michael smiled down at her and then looked up at me, eager to share the moment. His expression sobered when he saw my face.

"What's wrong?"

"I'll tell you later." I said. "Who wants to help make spaghetti?"

7

LEARNING TO PLAY

Looking on the bright side, we now had air conditioning. After several weeks of trying to make do with fans and closed blinds, we enjoyed the simple pleasure of closing the doors and windows and blasting the cool air. The PG&E bill would skyrocket, but for now it was a pleasure to sit and not sweat.

The AC did little to cool Michael down when I told him about the court-ordered visit with the birth parents. After the kids were tucked in bed, we retreated to our bedroom for a whispered but heated discussion.

"We should have known," Michael said. He paced about our bedroom, venting his frustration. "Louise must have been under pressure to get these kids placed, and we were the patsies. I feel like we've been tricked. These kids aren't adoptable because the birth parents are a headache. That's why the kids have been in so many foster homes."

I had to admit I, too, felt manipulated. The social worker may have planned this all along, moving the children into our home before revealing the fact that birth parent visits were still required by the courts. "Well, what do we do?" I asked. "You're not suggesting we give the kids back? They're just settling in. We have them registered for school, for god's sake!"

Michael stopped his pacing and we both went silent. How could we pack the kids up and return them to the emergency foster home? This past week I'd experienced being a mother for the first time. These kids had been disappointed and moved around so much in their short lives.

Was our home going to be just one more stop for them? I wiped tears from my eyes and prayed the children couldn't hear us.

"No, of course not, but we can't defy a court order. We're between a rock and a hard place." Michael slumped down on the bed. "What a mess!"

"Let's see if DSS can appeal the decision. They're still keeping our names and address from the birth parents so we shouldn't have any contact with them. Maybe this will blow over soon." As soon as I said this, I knew I was being naïve. We had no idea how these things worked.

The rest of the week went without incident. The children settled into their routines and were pretty cooperative at bedtime. Kayla got along well with Jenny, and even polished her nails one afternoon, but Robert was a source of irritation for her, especially when he didn't tidy up after himself in the bathroom. I didn't worry about that too much and asked Kayla to be patient.

I did worry about the children's lack of interest in playing. They were okay with it if I sat with them, but as soon as I stepped away they didn't know what to do. I had always thought kids preferred to play with each other or create their own little world. I knew I had as a kid. I built forts with my little brothers and pretended I was a schoolteacher with the neighborhood kids. There was none of that with Jenny and Robert. It was as if they were awaiting instructions for their every move.

One morning I thought I would get them started playing on their own by filling a couple of buckets with water on the back patio for some splashing around. The park pool had closed for the season and it was going to be another hot day. I retrieved the sand toys we'd purchased for the earlier outing at Del Valle and pulled some Tupperware and plastic measuring cups from kitchen drawers. I sat down on the patio steps and demonstrated what I thought would be a good time, pouring water into a plastic water can, dipping bowls into the buckets and filling measuring cups. I wanted them to know it was okay to get wet, have fun, and spray some water around. I got a giggle from Jenny when I sprayed her toes, but Robert just hopped back and frowned.

"You guys play here for a while. I'm going inside to sit down." I had to admit I was exhausted and hoped the kids would get the hang of this so I could get a break. With Michael back at work, it had been up to me to keep the kids occupied until school started. I was determined not to saddle Kayla with babysitting, though she was willing to help by watching the kids when I ran out for an errand. I was desperate for some downtime.

I put my feet up on the sofa, closed my eyes, and relished the cool air. When would things get easier? I fantasized a cozy domestic scene with the children playing quietly on the rug in front of the fireplace, and me, my feet up, book in hand and a glass of wine nearby. I tried to remember if I had ever seen June Cleaver or Donna Reed with their feet up on the couch. My eyes popped open and I realized I needed to check on the kids. I shouldn't have worried. Jenny and Robert were keeping an eye on me. Both their faces were pressed against the picture window, each encircled with their hands so they could peer through and see what I was up to.

8

Timmy and Company

On Sunday morning, we drove the children to their brother's foster home in Hayward. On the way over, Robert fidgeted with the seat belt and chewed his fingers as he stared out the window. We brought Jenny's baby doll along to keep her occupied, but she threw it on the floor and sulked. I did my best to reassure the children that this was only a visit and we would come pick them up later in the day. But when we arrived at the run-down foster home, a gloom settled over us. The brown stucco house was in need of repair and paint. Rotting leaves filled the gutters while weeds and dead shrubs lined the cracked front walk.

The middle-aged white man who answered the door frowned as he stepped back to let us in. He raked his longish brown hair back from his forehead, self-conscious of his appearance. His rock concert T-shirt, baggy shorts, and bare feet were what one would expect to see when interrupting a man at his home on a Sunday morning. From the newspapers spread on the floor beside a large easy chair in front of a loud television, it was apparent he had forgotten we were coming.

"Timmy's in the kitchen with the other kids. I'll go get him." He turned and walked off, not waiting for our response, but Timmy must have heard the doorbell because he ran into the room at full speed. He barreled toward Robert like a linebacker charging a quarterback. Michael stepped forward and grabbed Timmy as Robert hid behind me. Jenny prepared herself for the assault by clutching my leg and burying her face in my thigh.

"Timmy, get over here!" the man said. "We have to watch him with all the kids. He's a bruiser." Timmy sidled over to the man, giving Robert a warning look over his shoulder. He was a big kid for an eight-year-old. His sandy hair was wild from untamed cowlicks, like Robert's before his haircut. His face and shirt were smeared with pancake syrup and scrambled eggs. The jeans he wore were too small and torn and patched at the knee.

"Go put on a clean shirt and wash your face. Your parents will be here soon." The foster dad pointed Timmy toward the hall, then turned to us. "They'll be here in fifteen minutes. I heard you're not to meet them so you'd better get going. I'll keep an eye on these two till they come."

Robert and Jenny looked up at us. We didn't know this guy and we didn't know the birth parents other than the brief history we'd gotten from the social worker.

He noticed our hesitation, knitted his brow in annoyance, and then yelled into the kitchen. "Marsha, would you come in here and introduce yourself to these folks?" He turned back to me as his wife walked into the room wiping her hands on an apron. "You must be new to foster care. My wife and I have been doing this for almost ten years. You're going to have to get used to the birth parents being in the picture and learn to manage the visits yourself."

Michael and I glanced at each other. I wanted to explain we were fostering in order to adopt—that we weren't like them, doing it for income.

We didn't see Marsha's extended hand until she spoke. "Hi, how're you doing?" she said. The foster dad left the room to check on Timmy's progress while Marsha explained.

"Timmy's getting transferred at the end of the week to St. Vincent's School for Boys in Marin County. He needs more help than we can give him here. He's hurt both the little girls we're fostering. This means you'll have to find someplace else to meet the birth parents for the visit drop-offs from now on."

"Oh no, this is just this one time until the court order is reversed," I said. "We're adopting Jenny and Robert, and the birth parents' visits are supposed to stop."

Marsha looked at me blankly then chewed her lip.

"Well, that's fine then," she said. "Talk to your social worker about that. Now, let's say good-bye and get you two on your way."

We hugged Jenny and Robert and promised we would return at 4 p.m. to take them home. It was a strain to hide my distress from the children. I waited till I was in the car before I buried my face in my hands. "God, this is too hard."

Michael grimaced as he pulled away from the curb. "I can't help feeling like we've been pressured into something we can't get out of," he said. He pounded the steering wheel for emphasis. He turned and glared at me. "This is not what I signed up for."

He continued to grumble while I ignored him and worried about the children. Michael grew silent, perhaps realizing I wasn't going to argue with him. His mood grew dark as we drove back to Livermore past a monotonous view of parking lots, shopping centers, and apartments .

When we returned promptly that afternoon, the foster mother let us in.

"Well, you're on time," she said. "Let's not disturb my husband while he's watching the game." We saw him from the front door, settled in his easy chair drinking something from a can. "He works construction all week, so I try to keep the kids out of his hair on the weekends. Your kids are in the other room with the others. They've been here for a while."

We passed through a cluttered kitchen to a family room converted into a playroom filled with boxes of toys, wooden shelves of children's books, and kid-sized furniture. I was relieved to see Jenny and Robert seated on a rug in front of the television with Timmy. Two little girls, about the age of ten, sat on beanbag chairs in the corner and were braiding each other's hair. Jenny ran to us as soon as we came in, but Robert had his back turned to us, engrossed in an argument with Timmy. When Robert saw us and began to get up, Timmy slugged him. Robert winced, then backed away from his brother.

"Timmy, stop that," Marsha said. "Apologize to your brother." Timmy scowled and turned back to the television while Robert walked over to us, rubbing his arm.

"I'm sorry. That's one unhappy kid" she said. She lowered her voice as Timmy turned up the volume on the cartoon. "And his mood doesn't improve after he visits with his parents."

"What are they like?" I asked. I had to know what we were dealing with.

"Oh, they're all right, I guess." She cocked her head as if searching for the right words. "I really shouldn't be talking about this. After Timmy spends time with them, he seems anxious to start punching something. He'll be better off at St. Vincent's."

Jenny lifted her arms for me to pick her up and Robert stood behind Michael, still nursing his arm. I remembered the promise I had made to Robert about protecting him and understood now why he couldn't trust the promises adults made.

"You know, I shouldn't have said anything" she said. "I'm sure everything was just fine today. By the way, talk to your social worker about where you're dropping the kids off next Sunday, okay?" I mumbled my thanks and herded the kids out the front door. *We're not doing this every Sunday,* I thought to myself. *Why do they keep saying that?*

When I buckled the kids into the backseat of the Honda, I noticed that Jenny smelled sour and her shorts were soaked through. I'd provided two diapers in her backpack and they were still there, unused.

"We'll get you changed as soon as we get home, honey." I said. Trying to clean her up in the backseat of the car didn't seem practical. Jenny leaned her head against her car seat and stared out the window.

"Good, 'cause she stinks!" Robert said. He held his nose and looked disgusted.

"What did you two do all day?" I asked. I tried to sound nonchalant.

"We rode around in the car," Robert said. "And I'm hungry. Can we stop at McDonald's?" I reached into a grocery bag filled with snacks and fished out some fruit.

"Take the banana, Robert. We'll fix dinner when we get home," Michael said. "You couldn't have ridden around all day. Didn't you at least get out of the car to go to the bathroom or eat?"

"We went to lots of different houses. We stayed in the car while Daddy, Timmy, and Mom went inside. It was hot in the car and we didn't do anything." He sounded disappointed as he described his day. "They finally got me a big soda, and then I had to pee really bad. I knocked on the door of the house and no one answered so I went in the bushes." Robert looked embarrassed, as if confessing this might get him in trouble.

"Well, don't worry about that," I said. "Did they keep an eye on Timmy so he didn't hurt you?"

"When we first got in the car, Timmy kept hitting me and he pinched

Jenny until she cried so they put him up front. They took him inside with them when they visited their friends and left us in the car."

Robert lifted his shirt to show me welts turning into bruises.

I twisted around in my seat and saw that Jenny had fallen asleep, a small bruise showing below her sleeve.

"I'm sorry, Robert. It sounds like Timmy needs to learn how to be nicer."

"Well, I don't want to play with him anymore. When I see him next I'm going to punch him hard. He'll be sorry he messed with me."

We listened to Robert complain about his brother and plot his revenge. Once we got home, I bathed Jenny and dressed her in fresh clothes and a clean diaper while Robert helped Michael start dinner. Jenny followed me around all evening, clinging to my leg and climbing in my lap when I sat down. Robert went into his room after dinner, saying he was tired and needed to lie down. After a few minutes, Michael went to check on him and get him ready for bed. I heard Michael call me from the hall, his voice an urgent whisper. Robert was on the floor of his room, curled in a fetal position, weeping. Michael picked him up, put him in his bed, and rubbed his back, soothing him with humming. Robert buried his face in his pillow and sobbed.

After he fell asleep, I called Louise's voice mail and told her to contact me first thing the next day. She needed to call me at work, so I left that number as well as the home phone. My voice trembled as I described the events of the day, Timmy's abuse, the parent's neglect, and the children's reaction to this treatment. I told her what we needed: therapy for the children, reassurance that the family visits would be discontinued, and much more. I insisted she fix this situation immediately. I spoke too long and her machine cut me off. I called back and continued a second message, not caring if I sounded rude. I hoped she heard the outrage in my voice and not the helplessness I felt.

I'd made the calls from my desk in our bedroom. After I hung up the phone I stared out the window, clenching and unclenching my fists. I turned when I saw Michael's reflection behind me. He'd watched from the doorway and heard what I said. After a moment, he shook his head and walked down the hall.

9

BATHTUB SURPRISE

That's just perfect," I mumbled to myself, grateful no one was around while I listened to the social worker's message. Not only did the court hearing with the birth father result in the county backpedaling, but Louise was adamant that we help set up the next birth family visit and not jeopardize the county's case. She made no mention of how the children would be kept safe. How was I going to break this to Michael?

It was evening, the day after the first birth family visit. Kayla and Michael cooked dinner while Jenny and Robert played in their bedroom. It'd been a long day for everyone: Kayla and Robert's first day of school and my first day back to work. The kids were squabbling, and I could hear Michael barking orders to Kayla and her protesting. Our new routine was far from perfect.

The day had started out well with Michael making everyone's lunches while I got the two children up and dressed. I'd promised Kayla I'd drive her to school for her first day though it would make me late to my job in Manteca. Michael walked Robert to his classroom with Jenny in tow, then drove her to day care before going on to Hayward to work. We still had hopes of getting Jenny into special ed preschool, but she wasn't toilet-trained yet. The plan for the end of the day was that I'd pick Jenny up from day care while Michael collected Robert at his after-school day care before closing time at 6 p.m. Kayla would get herself home on the bus.

On the way to school, Kayla had fretted the whole way. "Everyone will have their own friends already and no one will like me," she said. "And what if I have the wrong clothes?" I kept my eyes on the road so I wouldn't betray my opinion of what Kayla was wearing. While most teen girls would have chosen their best outfit for the first day of school, Kayla selected a pair of worn jeans and a plain white blouse buttoned to the neck. She wore little makeup and her hair was pulled back in a messy pony tail. Though I was grateful she wasn't one of those kids who needed to rebel with wild outfits, she looked like she was going out of her way to be invisible. I wasn't exactly a snappy dresser myself and rarely wore more than a bit of lipstick, so I didn't think I could offer much advice. I hoped she'd make friends with other girls who might be a good influence in the style department.

After work, I drove from Manteca to Livermore to pick Jenny up from day care. Janice reported that Jenny cried for nearly an hour after Michael left and then fought with the other children most of the day. She wanted to be picked up and babied, and during lunch and snack time, she smeared food all over her face and clothes. I tried to apologize but Janice wouldn't have it.

"I understand Jenny's going to need some extra help, Catherine. We'll get through this together." I thanked her for her understanding and walked my messy, grumpy little girl out to the car.

"Momma," Jenny called from her bedroom, then yelped in pain. When I entered the children's room she was holding her hand. "Pee pee" she said and then pointed at a corner of the room near the sliding closet door. I looked to Robert for an explanation, but he shook his head and glared at Jenny. I walked over to where she pointed, bent over, then drew back in disgust, overwhelmed with the odor of urine.

"Robert, you have to clean this up. Come with me so we can get a bucket, towel, and scrub brush."

"But I didn't do anything!" he protested. I took his arm and led him to the garage for the cleaning supplies. As we passed through the kitchen, I informed the cooking crew that Robert had an accident that might delay dinner. While he cleaned up the mess, I turned my attention to Jenny sniffling and holding her hand.

"What's the matter, honey?" I asked. I examined a fresh welt turning purple. "Robert, did you hurt your sister?" I gave Jenny's hand a kiss and comforted her with a hug. He had his back to me while he scrubbed the carpet. He shook his head in denial and continued his task.

"You know you don't like it when your brother hurts you," I said. "Why do you think it's okay to hurt your sister?" He kept scrubbing and said nothing.

"Dinner's ready," Kayla said. She'd been standing in the doorway waiting for a chance to speak.

"Put that aside for now, Robert. Everybody wash their hands."

For the first time I noticed his jeans were sliced at the knees and the soles of one of his shoes flapped when he walked. "What happened to your shoe and your pants? They're brand new."

"I don't know. I guess they're getting worn out."

I noticed my scissors on his dresser. "These are my scissors, Robert. You need to ask permission if you want to borrow them. Have you been cutting your things?"

Robert stopped, looked at his shoes and pants as if seeing them for the first time, and then shook his head no. He wouldn't look at me. I put my hand on his shoulder and guided him to the dinner table.

The next morning, while I helped Jenny brush her teeth in our bathroom, Kayla rushed in. "You won't believe this," she said.

I helped Jenny down from her stepstool and followed Kayla to the hall bathroom. There she pointed to a tiny turd in the middle of the tub. I told Kayla to take her shower in our bathroom and headed to the kitchen where Michael and Robert were putting the lunches together.

"There's poop in the bathtub," I said. "I know I didn't do it, and I am pretty sure Kayla and Michael didn't either. Jenny has a hard time pooping anywhere but her diapers." Michael and I looked at Robert for an explanation but none came. "Robert, you need to clean up what you did in the bathtub. That isn't very nice for your sisters to find."

"But I didn't do it," he said. "Why are you picking on me? I think Kayla doesn't like me." Robert sniffed and looked at the floor.

Michael picked up a plastic sandwich bag and hurried to the bathroom, shouting over his shoulder as he left the room. "Your first job when you come home after school is scrubbing that bathtub till it's spotless."

Michael was running late so I finished bagging the lunches, handed Robert his, and packed mine in my briefcase by the door in the living room. I was about to ask Robert to stand by the front door and wait for Michael to walk him to school when I realized I was nervous about leaving him unsupervised, even for those few minutes. Robert's behaviors were clear signs he was distressed, and until we could get him to a therapist we had to watch him closely. I stood in the center of the room, paralyzed with the task of mentally reordering our careful routine. Jenny walked in carrying her pants and shoes. She'd pulled on her shirt by herself, but it was inside out. I finished helping her dress, then kissed her good-bye and told her to go find Daddy. I grabbed my briefcase, opened the front door, and took Robert's hand.

"Michael, I'm going to walk Robert to school today. Kayla, hurry—you're going to miss the bus."

10

THUG IN THE PARKING LOT

There was no getting around it. We were going to have to meet the birth parents and turn our children over to them for the entire Sunday. I was beside myself with outrage and anxiety, and I had difficulty hiding it from the children.

One evening as we prepared dinner, Michael and I discussed how we would go about dropping our children off with these people we'd never met, and in fact were afraid of. Not only were we concerned about the care the children were getting during these visits, but we were nervous about our own safety.

"We know he's been in prison several times, and she's been arrested for drug violations. What if they kidnap the kids?" Michael asked.

"I'm not so worried they won't bring the kids back. After all, they've been in foster care for almost three years. I'm more concerned Robert and Jenny will get hurt. If Robert is telling the truth, they're pretty negligent."

"Maybe you're right—maybe they don't want the kids. But tell me … we want to remain anonymous, right? How are we supposed to do that if we're meeting them face to face?" He stopped chopping vegetables and turned to me for ideas.

"We have to tell Robert not to mention our names or where we live. What else can we do?"

We chose the drop-off place: a Carl's Jr parking lot located in the nearby town of Dublin. The spot was out in the open and busy with traffic and pedestrians; we'd figured that would make it easier to get help if we needed it. It also had a restroom in case we had a long wait. I looked up the address and left the information with the social worker so she could tell the birth parents where to show up. After we dropped the kids off, we planned to distract ourselves by taking Kayla to a movie.

The day was forecast to be another scorcher, so I made sure Jenny had a hat and I smeared sun block on them both. We packed their swimming suits for what Louise had told us would be a day at a lake. During the short drive to Dublin I promised the kids we were going to do something fun when they returned. They needed to know we'd be there at the end of the day to take them home.

"Let's do a barbecue tonight, guys. Do you want hamburgers or hot dogs?"

Robert stared out the car window. "Hot dogs, I guess," he said.

"Hot dogs," Jenny said. All of us looked at her in surprise. Even Michael glanced around before returning to his driving.

"You can say 'hot dogs,' Jenny. Good for you! Hot dogs it is then," I said. Jenny beamed.

We pulled into the parking lot and Robert spotted his birth parents right away. We maneuvered into a spot parallel to their rust-colored four-door Chevy. A plump woman in her late twenties exited the passenger side of the car and walked toward us. She smiled and waved at the kids in the backseat. I noticed teeth missing. The woman's long hair swung into Jenny's face as she bent to pull her out of her car seat. I got out to help, but she'd already scooped Jenny up while Robert exited on his own. The driver of the car stayed seated and didn't look at the children or at us. His face was obscured by aviator sunglasses and shoulder-length red hair. When he became aware of me standing next to him, he turned toward the backseat where Robert was buckling himself in.

"Where's Timmy?" Robert asked.

"We'll pick him up next. Don't worry about it," the man said. His tone was gruff—unnecessarily so, I thought, for such a simple question.

"Mind your daddy, Robert," the woman said. She closed the car door for Robert and walked to the other side with Jenny on her hip. Jenny looked alarmed, twisted around, and reached her arms toward me. "Momma?" she said.

My heart leapt to my throat, and it was all I could do to keep from running up and snatching her back from this stranger. "Honey, you go have fun today and we'll pick you up later and take you home." The woman ignored me and fastened Jenny in next to her brother.

Robert watched us from the rear window as they drove off, then turned around abruptly, as if obeying an order from the front seat.

I opened the car door and sank into the passenger seat, leaning back against the headrest for a moment, sick at heart. I fought back tears as I reached over to close the car door, but found it blocked by someone who had come up behind me. A woman, whom I mistook for a man at first, leaned down into my face, waved an identification badge, and pulled out some official-looking papers.

"I represent the attorney for the children's parents. These are papers that require you to give us your name and address so you can be properly served."

"Who are you, and why are you bothering us?" I said. I pulled away from her and tugged on the door. She blocked the car door with her hip and wouldn't budge.

"I just told you. I work for the parents. You're going to be deposed so we need your name and address."

"I don't have to tell you anything." I looked wide-eyed at Michael, willing him to start the car. "Get out of the way." I said to the woman. Michael eased our Honda forward so I could close the door. I slammed it hard, not caring if I smashed her hand. She shouted at us as we drove off.

"Oh, God, this is awful! I think they've hired people to harass us!" I said.

Michael had nearly pulled out in front of oncoming traffic in his haste to get out of the parking lot. I struggled to put on my seat belt and realized I'd snagged it in the door.

"What if they find out where we live?" Michael asked. "They could send people to hurt us. He's been in prison. He knows people."

"I know! DSS can't protect us—that was a lie. They're trying to intimidate us, and we may need a lawyer or a restraining order or something. Should we call the police?" My imagination was running wild, and I began to worry if the children really were being kidnapped after all.

When we arrived home we tried desperately to get through to DSS using the emergency numbers we'd been given, but all we got were voice mails. We left several messages, but no one returned our call.

We gave up the plan of going to a movie. We were too anxious to enjoy it and wanted to be around in case someone from DSS called back. We spent the afternoon fretting about what to do, and not hearing from Social Services, and then we headed back to the parking lot for the 4 p.m. pickup time. We were hoping the children would be returned as promised and worried we would encounter the thug who'd bothered us earlier. We waited across the street until we saw their Chevy pull into the parking lot. This time the woman was driving and the man was nowhere in sight. Robert was in the front seat and Jenny was in a car seat in the back. Both were still in their swimming suits with towels wrapped around them. Jenny had fallen asleep, so the mother jostled her awake as she unbuckled her from the car seat. I moved next to her to take Jenny from her.

"So what's the deal with you sending someone to get our information?" I said. "I thought everyone was making an effort to be cooperative here." I was taller than she was and was feeling bolder because her creepy husband wasn't around.

"You'll have to speak to our attorney about that." She shouted this as she climbed back in the driver's seat and slammed her door shut.

Like the last time, Jenny was soggy, smelly, and glassy-eyed with exhaustion. I positioned my vanity mirror so Robert could see me and asked him about his day.

"We went to a lake. Jenny started to float away and Daddy had to swim fast to catch her.

Then Timmy shoved me down on some rocks and I was bleeding, see?" He pulled up his shirt to show a gash that was still bloody and filled with grit. I turned around to inspect the damage. Robert relayed his experience in a matter-of-fact way, though he knew I would be distressed by it.

"Oh, honey, I'm sorry. That looks like it hurts. I'll take care of that when we get home."

"Daddy said I was being a crybaby. That I should stand up for myself and not be such a wimp. I kicked Timmy later and Daddy got mad."

"Oh, dear." I glanced at Michael to see if he was listening. "Well, what did you have for lunch?"

"I had to split french fries with Timmy and he got more than me."

Robert's story took a turn toward self-pity, and I had no way of knowing whether his version was true, but it didn't matter. It was clear he was unhappy with the day and worried about his safety.

Jenny woke up and whimpered in discomfort, reaching for me from her car seat.

"We're almost home, honey," I said. "We're almost there."

11

LOONEY TUNES

These visits have to stop." I said. "Not only are the children being neglected, I think they're distressed from the confusion of this back and forth with us and their birth parents. It has to be tough for them."

"And this kills our weekend," Michael said. "Sunday is the only chance we have to spend quality time with the kids—otherwise we're just their babysitters, shuffling them back and forth to school."

"Maybe there's a way around this. What if we said we had plans for Sunday and ask for an exception? Or maybe one of the children has the sniffles and we skip a week? There's got to be something we could do until the county gets the ruling reversed."

It was the Tuesday evening after the children's disastrous birth family visit and our encounter with the attorney's thug. Louise had given me a referral for a children's advocate attorney, but she had no advice for Michael and me except to continue to comply with the court order and document our experience. I got the message that we were to do as we were told.

"We might be able to get the visits stopped, or at least supervised, if we prove they're hurting the kids," I said. "The children's psychologist needs to know everything that happens. Then we can get her to make a recommendation for the judge."

Michael looked dubious. "She won't lie for us."

"With the problems the kids are having, she won't have to."

Proving the birth family visits were harmful was not going to be that hard. Physically, the children were returned in bad shape. Both kids were dehydrated, hungry, and sunburned from the day at the lake. Jenny clung to me all evening and cried when Michael dropped her off at day care the next day. Janice reported she'd been fighting with the other children and throwing her food on the floor.

Robert wasn't faring too much better. He stole my scissors from my desk drawer, cut holes in his new jacket, and snipped sections of his hair. Later that evening, Kayla found urine in a plastic cup we kept in the bathroom.

The stress in the household from these visits affected Kayla as well. Michael overheard a phone call to her mother, complaining about school and the lack of attention she got from us. When Michael asked her about it, she burst into tears and accused him of spying on her. Later she asked me if I'd drive her to school because kids on the bus were harassing her.

A call from the children's attorney was the one ray of hope in the week. Rick Sanchez listened patiently while I described the condition of the children after the birth family visits. I complained that we were disappointed the kids couldn't be adopted yet and that it was unfair to have to turn our kids over to these people every Sunday. When I told him about the thug who tried to intimidate us, he had lots of questions.

"You didn't say anything, did you?" he asked.

"No, not at all, but she said she would find out who we were and where we lived and we would be subpoenaed to appear in court."

"It sounds like you guys need an attorney too, Catherine. I have a colleague who may be able to take this on. The county should reimburse you for attorney's fees. Can I come by and talk to Robert about how he's feeling about all this? Tomorrow afternoon around four would work for me."

"Sure." That would mean asking my boss for another afternoon off. I'd already taken off for our first appointment with the children's therapist and planned to ask my boss about coming in later so I could take Kayla to school. I hoped he'd continue to be understanding about all this.

"Rick, until we get the judge to reverse his order for these visits, can we get out of them somehow? What if we said we had travel plans for this coming Sunday and skip this next visit?"

"That might work. Give it a try . . . and you didn't hear that from me." He chuckled as he hung up the phone.

When I met Rick the next day, I couldn't help but be charmed. A short, stocky, balding man, he wore an outrageous green tie decorated with the Tasmanian Devil cartoon.

"Like the tie?" he asked. He flipped it up at me as I let him in.

"Sure. Nice touch."

"Hey, you must be Robert." Rick shook hands with my little boy, who was hovering nearby.

"This is the man I told you about. It's okay to talk to him about anything you want, and he wants to hear how you're feeling about the visits with your brother and your birth parents."

"How about we go into the dining room for a talk, Robert? You okay with that?" Robert nodded and followed him to the table. I busied myself in the nearby family room, trying not to appear like I was eavesdropping.

I overheard Rick's questions about the visits, his brother, and the birth parents, but I couldn't hear Robert's murmured responses. I hoped Robert wouldn't change his story. There was always a chance he felt like he was tattling on his birth parents and didn't want to get them into trouble.

Rick and I conferred on the front porch after the interview. "Do you think Robert is telling the truth?" I asked. "It's hard to believe some of what he said, but if any of it's true, it's only a matter of time before the kids get hurt."

"Does it really matter if everything is totally true?" Rick asked. "What's important is he's scared when he's with them and he's letting us know they can't be trusted to take care of him. If you share with the psychologist how the children look and behave after these visits and get her to make a recommendation, we have a strong case to reduce the frequency of the visits and require supervision."

"That's it? Just get them reduced? I don't want to do this at all anymore."

"Look, one thing at a time. I saw the records from previous visits. Their last foster home had to take the kids to the emergency room with severe sunburn after one of their visits. At least they're consistent in their neglect."

I groaned. What needed to happen for someone to pay attention here? "What about somebody harassing us?" I asked. "They're trying to get our identities, and we're worried they're going to show up here and take the kids."

"Tell me what happened again." I repeated the story of last Sunday's scare while he nodded.

"That's good," he said. He seemed happy about what had happened.

"I'm having a hard time seeing what's good about this," I said.

"Don't you know when we've hit the jackpot?"

I walked with Rick to his car. "I don't understand."

"I am going to love bringing this to the judge's attention after he's ordered your anonymity. Call my buddy so you have legal representation. You're going on the stand, Catherine. This is going to be a lot more fun than I thought."

12

TAKING A HIKE

I left the message at a time when I knew I would get her voice mail. I worked on the wording in advance. It went something like *We had plans for a camping trip weeks ago before we knew about the court order. If we cancel we'll lose the reservation fee.* It was a lie and I didn't care. Louise was going to have to tell the birth parents we weren't available for their Sunday visit, and she'd have to get permission from the judge for the exception. I didn't plan on answering the phone if she called back, and we had a lot of packing to do.

We wanted our first camping trip with the kids to be memorable: cooking over a Coleman stove, making a campfire, roasting s'mores, and lots of hiking. We already had most of the gear, including an extra tent and sleeping bags for the kids. We assembled a first aid kit, found extra flashlights, and made a grocery list that included lots of junk food. We gathered all the things we wanted to take in a large pile in the middle of the garage—and realized it wasn't all going to fit in the Honda.

We considered taking two vehicles, with Michael driving his Datsun pickup with the camping gear and me following with the children in the Honda. But the thought of driving both vehicles to a local campground for an overnight stay seemed ridiculous: we could make it all fit if we organized ourselves better. We packed the big stuff like the Coleman stove, lantern, boxes of food, and wood in the trunk. The cooler separated the kids in the backseat, and the two tents, sleeping bags, pillows, and blankets were stuffed around the children and at their feet.

Michael and I couldn't help making wisecracks about how funny we looked.

"California Okies, that's what we are," he said. He closed the trunk carefully so the lawn chairs wouldn't smash the food. "I hope we can get into the campsite before most of the other campers get there. They might take up a collection."

"What are Okies?" Robert asked. He looked worried as we helped him buckle up amid all the pillows.

"That's a word from a long time ago," I said. "People who had to travel a long way across country had to pack all their belongings in their cars. We're just kidding."

"Okay, but have you been camping before? Do we have enough food? I don't think Jenny's going to like camping." I was beginning to understand Robert's anxieties. Through his eyes, we were just another set of clueless adults marching toward disaster.

"We have plenty of food. Don't worry. And we've been camping many times so we know all about it. Maybe you can help me build the campfire tonight."

"I know how to do that already. I'll show you." He settled back in his seat, satisfied he would provide me with a lesson later. Michael laughed. He'd learned a long time ago that no one showed this old Girl Scout how to build a campfire.

Kayla shook her head in amazement as I climbed in and packed diapers under my seat. "You guys look like a clown car from the circus." She waved us off, relieved to have some time for herself.

"What's a clown car?" Robert asked.

When we arrived at the campsite, we were glad to find it wasn't crowded. Though the hills and grass were dry from the rainless summer, the trees were starting to change to their fall color and there was a chill in the air. Our campsite was shaded by a golden-leafed sycamore. We all helped pitch the two tents. Jenny wanted to play house in the tent and got the giggles as she peeked out through the tent flap. Michael unfolded our lawn chairs near the picnic table and I settled into one, eager to relax and enjoy a *Sunset* magazine I'd packed away. Jenny and Robert stood before us waiting for instructions about what to do next.

"Momma … potty." Jenny dragged me toward the outhouse near our campsite.

While we were gone, Michael showed Robert a field guide to birds and found a picture of the stellar jay that was looking for a handout on our picnic table.

When we returned I rummaged in the kitchen box for a trash bag for the dirty diaper and helped wash Jenny's hands at the spigot. "I think you guys need a hike," I said. I turned to Michael. "Why don't I take them first, we'll have lunch, and you can go exploring with them after that. If we go in shifts, we can each get a break."

"Sounds like a plan." Michael was happy for the rest and retrieved a library book he'd stuffed into the glove box. I heard the pop of his soda can as we headed down the dusty road.

"Let's see how many animals we can find. Everything counts—bugs, birds, lizards. If you see a snake, let me look at it first. We don't want to scare anything and we don't hurt any animals, agreed?" Jenny held my hand while Robert followed. Just off the road we came to two trailheads, and I calculated how long we could walk before we needed to turn around for lunch. I wanted my time in the lawn chair too.

"Let's try this one." I said. My selection must have sounded arbitrary because Robert stopped in his tracks and looked worried.

"You mean you're not sure that's the right way to go?" he asked.

"Well, there isn't a right way, Robert. We can choose any one we want."

"But I thought you knew where you were going. What if we get lost?"

"It would be pretty hard to get lost around here. There are a lot of people nearby and the park's not that big. We'll be fine." I started walking, but Robert lagged behind.

"Would you like to be the leader?" I asked. "Maybe you can find some bugs or birds first and teach Jenny new words."

Robert brightened up and squared his shoulders as he squeezed by me to take the lead. "Here're some walking sticks," he said. He ran under a nearby tree and picked through fallen branches till he found one the right size. "Follow me." It was heartening to see Robert's anxiety dissolve when I placed him in charge, though I wished he had more confidence in me.

We returned an hour later to the campsite bearing colored leaves, a caterpillar, and pretty rocks Robert had collected near the creek bed. We'd seen ducks, wild turkeys, a flock of Canada geese, and lots of ground squirrels and lizards. We had tossed the walking sticks in the creek along with big stones that made a satisfying *kerplunk* as they hit the water. I was pooped and ready for lunch, happy to see that Michael had made sandwiches while we were gone. Later I lay down in the tent with Jenny for a short nap while Michael took Robert for another hike.

Dinner was spaghetti cooked on the Coleman stove, French bread, and carrot sticks. Robert helped me look for kindling, and together we built a campfire of the logs we had brought along from our fireplace at home. We roasted marshmallows on straightened coat hangers and smashed the goo between graham crackers and chocolate for s'mores. We tried some campfire songs until it was time for bed. We wiped the children's faces as best we could and helped them brush their teeth and get in their jammies. Michael read them a story while I packed our food in the car, safe from the raccoons. The kids played in one of the tents with their flashlights while Michael and I talked by the fire.

"What do you think's going to happen?" Michael asked. He was worried about the court order and the consequences of our taking off for the weekend.

"I don't think anything bad is going to happen. Louise said the court will allow this exception. What I'm more worried about is how we're going to juggle all the stuff the kids need with both of us working these full-time jobs. I've taken a lot of time off work lately."

"We can't afford any cut in income, and I'm not due for any raises at the gallery."

"I know, but I was thinking of working the Manteca job on contract, work from home and maybe take on another client while the kids are in school. Megan said her boss is looking for an outside salesperson for commercial landscaping."

"Are you sure you can juggle all that? Will you be able to earn as much with the two jobs?"

"Something's got to give," I said. "Besides, Jenny will be starting preschool soon, and someone has to be home to meet the bus."

"I can't do it. Maybe Kayla can help more?"

"We promised we wouldn't load her down this year. Let's give this plan a try."

I paused before continuing. "So, I have another thing for us to discuss." I had learned it was better to wait till Michael was relaxed before hitting him with problems, but sometimes there were too many things to deal with. "I spoke to the attorney that Rick Sanchez thought we should hire. He charges a hundred fifty an hour."

"We'll never be able to afford that. Won't the county pay for it?"

"He's going to see if he can get appointed by the court to work for us. Counting him, that'll be four attorneys involved."

"Well that's just great. This is getting so complicated and expensive. A foreign adoption would have been a breeze in comparison to what we're going through now."

We both stared at the fire, watching the wood pop and sparks fly. It seemed like years had passed since that first camping trip when we had dreamed that children would make our lives more complete. We'd had no way of knowing then that our dream would include sinking into debt and preparing for a court battle.

13

New Things to Learn

As Halloween neared, we decorated our windows with cardboard pumpkins and skeletons and school drawings of witches. Michael showed the kids how to clean out and carve a pumpkin, piling goop on newspapers laid out on the children's kitchen table. There was a lot of discussion about what kind of candy to pass out, with everyone picking their favorites in the hope some of it would be left over. Robert wanted to be a ghost, so Michael tie-dyed a sheet and helped him pick out creepy makeup. Jenny and I went to Target and selected a little devil costume complete with red cape, horns, and a pitchfork. Robert had a party to go to, and Michael accompanied him while Jenny and I went around the neighborhood.

To help Jenny get confidence with trick-or-treating, we had a few practice runs at the front door. She rang the doorbell, smiled sweetly, and opened her bag for a deposit. I figured that was close enough so we headed out to the neighborhood, starting a couple of blocks from our home. At the first house I stood a few yards back while Jenny rang the doorbell and tried her routine. The woman who answered her door and gave Jenny candy was startled to receive a warm hug and wet kiss in thanks.

"Bye, Mama," Jenny said. She waved to the lady and ran to show me what she'd gotten. I smiled and nodded at the woman standing stunned at her front door, then knelt to speak to Jenny.

"Honey, remember what I told you about hugs and kisses? Those are special and only for family." Jenny scanned my face for signs she'd done something wrong. My little girl was smart enough to hedge her bets with every woman she came across. I had to admire the street smarts.

"It's okay if you forget. I'm not mad. Show me what candy you got." She pulled out what she'd collected at the first house. "That's great. Now remember, if anyone gives you candy, all you have to do is say *thank you*. No kisses, okay?" Jenny nodded and hugged me, seeking reassurance. We finished our trick-or-treating with me hovering close as a bodyguard.

Doling out affection wasn't the only strategy our children must have employed during their early foster experiences. We learned in our parenting classes that foster kids often worry about food. Jenny hoarded her dinner in her cheeks while she ate, and we often found food stuffed under her mattress. Robert was a picky eater, refusing to eat anything that seemed foreign to him. Michael and I hoped regular dinners together would lessen these anxieties and help us bond as a family.

During the workweek, we settled into a routine, with Kayla and Jenny setting the table and Michael and Robert fixing dinner. Robert became more adventurous with food once he felt he was in charge of the menu planning and preparation. I did my part by cleaning up after the meal with help from the kids. We also used dinner time to share about our day and help Jenny learn a few words.

"Potatoes, Jenny. Can you say potatoes?" I asked. She was perched on the step stool that doubled as her high chair, pointing to a bowl of mashed potatoes just out of reach. Her mouth was stuffed with bread she had grabbed when she first sat down.

"Toes," she said. It was the best she could do and it was close enough. "Good job, Jenny," I said. I piled the potatoes on her plate.

"Yay!" said Kayla, clapping like a cheerleader. What a sweetheart.

"Big deal," said Robert.

"Let her try," Michael said. "She has to learn new words."

"She's just a baby. She can't talk yet." Robert scowled and sat back in his chair. Maybe a Jenny who didn't need him as interpreter was a change he wasn't prepared for.

Michael caught my eye while he served up the peas.

"Sure she can. Why don't you tell her the names of the food? Say the words slowly so she can learn."

Robert blinked and sat up straight. He surveyed the table, considering the new idea of being the teacher.

"These are easy. Say peas." He pointed at the vegetables and nodded encouragement.

Jenny looked at Robert solemnly and tried to repeat each item as he instructed until she tired of the game and went back to chewing and smiling.

The following Monday when I arrived home from the job in Manteca, everyone was in the kitchen helping make supper—toasted cheese sandwiches and tomato soup. Michael and Kayla carried plates laden with full soup bowls to the dining table.

"Jenny has a lot to tell us," Michael said. "She's been chatting non-stop." Today had been her first day at the special education preschool.

Jenny climbed onto the step stool while I fastened a towel around her neck to keep her clothes clean. "How was school today, Jenny?" I asked. I wasn't really expecting a full rundown, but I treated her like any member of the family who had something to share.

"Oooh, aaah," she said. She threw both arms up and gestured wildly, drawing pictures in the air with her own version of sign language.

"Oh, my. Did you have fun at school today, honey?" I asked.

Jenny clapped her hands in delight, hopped up out of her seat, and fell face first into her soup. When she looked up she was coated with cream of tomato. Her surprised look turned sad when she saw Robert laughing and pointing. She wailed with embarrassment. Michael and I struggled to remain straight-faced as we settled her back on the stool and mopped up the mess. Kayla held both hands over her mouth to control her giggles.

"Jenny, we are so happy you like school." Michael said. I kissed her on the forehead while I pinned on a clean towel. Jenny mustered one of her sunny smiles, happy for the attention.

"Kayla, why don't you tell us about your day now," I said.

"I don't know. That was a hard act to follow."

14

Keep On Smiling

As I stood in the doorway to the children's bedroom, Jenny pushed by me, clutching the clothes she planned to wear. Robert lay in bed, his face turned to the window.

"Robert, please get up. Your breakfast is on the table and you need to be at school in thirty minutes," I said.

He turned toward me, wiping his nose on his pajama sleeve. "I hate school. I don't want to go. Nobody likes me."

"I'll see you later." Michael shouted something about picking up the cleaning as the door slammed behind him. Did he say he would pick up the cleaning or he wanted me to?

Kayla rushed up to me wide-eyed and breathless. "Have you seen my black turtleneck? It was drying on the back of the dining room chair with my other sweaters."

"They're all in your drawer. I put them away earlier. Would you check on Jenny? She just headed off in the direction of the kitchen and she looks like she needs help getting dressed." Kayla stopped her dash back to her room, groaned, and went to look for her sister. We both knew she had a bus to catch.

I sat beside Robert on his bed and rubbed his back. I could feel his ribs under his pajamas. "What's going on?"

"None of the other kids like me. I don't want to go to school."

It was a Monday—after another of those dreadful birth family visits. The experience had been a disappointment to him. His birth parents had made vague promises about the family all living together again, but then ignored him during the time they were together. Robert had cried himself to sleep. I had no sympathy for these thoughtless people who kept our children from enjoying their new life with us.

I tried to distract him. "I saw a bird on the fence and I don't know what kind it is. Shall we get the binoculars and see if we can figure it out?" Robert sat up and sniffed. "Okay."

This was my first day working from home as a contractor. My boss had approved the idea when I showed how he could save money on benefits, and I knew he was trying to accommodate me and my new family situation. For his part, Michael was not happy with the resulting cut in income.

We had reorganized our morning routine so I could start my East Coast calls before the kids were up. I'd thought an hour was all I needed to get everyone out the door, but I hadn't anticipated this problem with Robert.

I wondered if Michael had noticed that Robert wasn't up and had just left it for me to handle.

"Kayla, don't miss your bus." She ran from her bedroom, grabbed her lunch, and darted out the front door with only one arm in her windbreaker. "Jenny's almost dressed," she said over her shoulder.

"Come back if you miss the bus—and thanks." The door slammed so I wasn't sure if she heard me.

In her bedroom Jenny tugged at the clothes Kayla helped her pick out, a pink and yellow jersey outfit. I straightened her pants and fastened the Velcro snaps of her sturdy shoes. As I helped her brush her teeth and comb her hair, I called to Robert, "Are you dressed? We only have a few minutes to look for birds."

The doorbell rang. I peered through the peephole to find a small woman glaring straight at me through the viewer. When I opened the door she stuck an envelope in my face. "Catherine Sievert?"

"Well … yes. Who are you?" When people assumed I had the same last name as my husband, I didn't bother to correct them.

"You've been served. Good day." She was off the porch and down our front walk before I could respond. I closed the door, opened the envelope, and saw enough to know I held a summons. We were being deposed by the birth parents' attorney. This meant they knew where we lived now.

My shoulders tensed and a headache began to creep up my neck.

"Can we go bird watching now?" Robert tugged at my elbow and held up the binoculars.

"All right, but let's get you a banana so you can eat it on your way to school." I put the summons on my desk, which was now in the living room, heaped with customer files and lists of prospects. I helped Robert adjust the binoculars so he could see the house finch perched on the fence, and we looked up "house finch" in the bird book.

Jenny and I walked Robert to his classroom after getting a late pass from the principal's office and then waited for her bus to arrive in the driveway.

When I got back to my desk, I took a moment to be grateful I was home instead of commuting to Manteca. The morning chaos would have been much worse if I had to worry about the highway traffic and getting to an office on time. I scanned the summons to confirm my suspicions and made a note in my calendar of the date and location of the deposition. There was no use putting off calling the attorney Rick had recommended. That task went on my to-do list for the day along with a half dozen other urgent items. I rubbed my neck and rolled my shoulders, hoping the kink would release. I could sit here and feel sorry for myself or I could get to work. I felt the weight of my employer's trust and the need for the income, so there was no use putting off what to do next.

I made a decent living selling refurbished computer parts, but it was dreary work. I succeeded because I was disciplined and reliable. I made at least ten calls an hour, more if possible. Each took time because I documented what the customer needed and any prices I quoted and then scheduled the callback in my tickler file. My customers relied on me to make sure their orders were problem free. My boss trusted me to make the calls despite any distractions at home.

I was accustomed to people relying on me, and I rarely said no when anyone needed my help. When I was young, Sunday Mass had included sermons about service and self-sacrifice. *God never gives you more than you can handle* was supposed to be a comfort for the trials of daily life. As the oldest of six children, I was responsible for my brothers' and sisters' care as well as most of the housework. In high school, I was elected president of several clubs and led my Girl Scout troop to organize a summer camp for underprivileged kids. I'd always been the "go to" person in tough situations and relished that reputation. But today, with my work piled in front of me, the responsibility of caring for these children, and the prospect of a court battle, my confidence wavered.

I pulled out the file for the next customer, cushioned the receiver between my ear and the stiff shoulder and dialed, remembering to smile as I waited for him to answer. I'd learned early on it's important to smile when talking on the phone. People can hear it in your voice.

15

GIRDING FOR BATTLE

The room next to the Alameda County family court was windowless and furnished with a mix of scarred wooden tables and mismatched chairs. The attorney for the birth parents, a gaunt woman with spikey blond hair, was engrossed in her notes and didn't look up when we came in. She scribbled on her notebook, the padded shoulders of her polyester suit jacket bunched up around her neck. A milk crate filled with manila folders was lashed to a luggage tote on the floor next to her. When she finally looked up, she pointed to a seat opposite her, then arched her eyebrows when she saw I wasn't alone. David Haversham, the attorney the children's lawyer had recommended, was dressed in Brooks Brothers and polished oxfords and carried a leather briefcase with a combination lock. He nodded to her, pulled my chair out for me, and waited for me to get settled before finding a seat for himself. He smiled at the court reporter when she entered the room and she smiled back at his familiar face.

The birth parents' attorney, Lynn Cutler, flashed a smile that on anyone else would have been welcoming. "We're just here to get some information in preparation for the court hearing. Are you comfortable, Mrs. Sievert?"

"I'm fine."

"Good."

"Actually, the name on the summons is not my legal name," I said. I thought I would clear that up right away. Nothing like finding a mistake to throw your adversary off her game.

"Oh, I see. We need to fix our records then. Let's get you sworn in with your correct name, and then we'll get started."

She checked her notes while I repeated the oath the court reporter read.

"So let's clear this up. Your husband is Michael Sievert, right?"

"Yes."

"You're the county's foster parents for Robert and Jenny Clyde, right?"

"Yes."

"Did the county tell you the children were eligible for adoption?"

"Yes."

"And you all live in Livermore at your home on 4516 Sherman Oaks Avenue?"

My jaw tightened as I chafed at putting our address on record. I hesitated and looked at Dave. He nodded for me to answer.

"The location of our home was to remain secret, but yes."

"Ms. Marshall, you don't have to be nervous."

"I'm not nervous. I'm just answering your questions."

She continued to read down her list and I answered each the way I'd been coached by Dave and Rick. We got to questions about the birth family visits, and she zeroed in on the time we took the kids camping instead.

"We understand you refused to take the children to visit with their parents on October fifteenth, is that right?"

"I didn't refuse. We had other plans for that weekend. The judge allowed it."

I looked her in the eye and smiled for the first time, just as warmly as she'd smiled at me earlier. We both knew that wasn't exactly what happened, and she seemed to be calculating how far she could push it. I said nothing while I waited for her next question.

"I hope you plan on cooperating with these family visits."

Since she hadn't asked me a question, I didn't respond. I kept my gaze steady and settled back in my chair. Dave had warned she might try to bait me into going on the defensive. The court reporter's fingers hovered over her machine.

Dave broke the standoff. "I hope we're near the end of your questions, Lynn. Ms. Marshall has taken off work to be here."

Their attorney checked her notes and continued. "You recall meeting our agent during a family visit drop off on September twelfth?"

"At the time I didn't know she was your agent. Someone just approached our car and began asking a lot of questions."

"She presented identification and indicated she worked for me, right?"

"When I asked for it."

"Ms. Marshall, there's no need to be hostile." In fact, I had a lot of reasons to be hostile, and I resented being dragged in for questioning, but I wasn't going to let her get the better of me.

"She's just answering your questions, Lynn. Can you get to the point?" I could see Dave was getting irritated, or at least pretending to be. The less I said the better. Both Dave and Rick had advised me I didn't have to let anyone know how I felt about the harassment we were receiving. We could save that for the hearing if the judge allowed me to speak.

"I think it's important that Ms. Marshall know we meant no harm. We just needed the information for this deposition."

"If the judge wanted you to have their names, he would have given them to you," Dave said. "You were out of line sending a private eye to harass them." His pencil drilled into his tablet for emphasis, and the reporter recorded his comments.

Her eyes narrowed as she looked from Dave to me. What did she expect? Perhaps she was surprised that we had hired our own attorney and that I was prepared for this meeting. She fumbled through her files as if she were looking for more questions. "I guess we're done here," she said.

As Dave and I rose to leave, I glanced at him to gauge how I'd done, but he didn't look at me. We walked out of the room, through the hall, and down the elevator without a word, careful in case we were being observed. It wasn't until we were back in his car that I let myself relax. "How'd I do?" I asked.

"Perfect, and you're going to do fine at the court hearing," Dave said. "We've got them worried."

"Good, because I think I'm getting the hang of this."

16

THE TRUE COST OF ADOPTION

The closest I'd come to a courtroom was what I'd seen on TV, so I was surprised by the cheery light oak and bright colors of the Alameda Family Court. The gallery section was deserted, but the area around the judge's bench bustled with activity. Everybody seemed engrossed in conversation, heads bent together and taking notes. I hesitated at the gate, but Dave held it open for me so I could sit with him at the plaintiff's table. I didn't see enough room for me because it was already crowded; Rick, the children's attorney, someone from DSS, and the agency's attorney were all there.

Rick greeted Dave with a good-natured punch. Dave chuckled, rubbed his shoulder in mock pain and then introduced me to the county people while Rick asked the bailiff about more chairs. I pulled one up to the table and squeezed in. No cartoon ties for him today—Rick wore a sedate, brown-striped number with a tweed jacket and wrinkled Dockers.

The birth mother's sweatshirt, jeans, and sandals struck me as inappropriate, but I guessed she was going for the "poor me" look that might win her sympathy. Her attorney, a thin young man in an ill-fitting suit, tried to engage her in preparation while she picked at a string on the cuff of her pants. Lisa Clyde now had her own attorney, for reasons soon apparent.

Everyone turned when Timothy Clyde entered, shackled and clad in an orange jumpsuit and chaperoned by a deputy. On the drive to the courthouse Dave had told me his parole had been revoked after an alcohol-fueled altercation with a traffic cop. I assumed this turn of events was in our favor.

Rick shared his opinion with us in a loud whisper. "Nothing like showing up in prison orange when you're trying to convince the judge you can be a good parent."

"This explains why he wasn't at the first supervised family visit last week," I said. "Lisa told the kids he was sick." The birth family visits were now supervised by a social worker, thanks to the recommendation of the children's therapist.

The three of us glanced at the opposite table, now as crowded as ours with the attorneys, the birth parents, and the deputy squeezed in behind them. Timothy Clyde slumped in his seat like he was settling in to watch a ball game. The deputy poked him to stand when the bailiff announced the judge. It took him a moment to gather up his shackles and get out of his chair.

The judge looked like a TV star with a full head of white hair, flashy teeth, and a tan. He hopped up to the bench, settled in, and surveyed the crowded tables before him. I may have imagined a weariness briefly clouding his eyes, but then he got down to business. He asked the court clerk to confirm the purpose of the hearing and began asking questions. "I see you're representing the foster parents, Mr. Haversham. Are they present?"

David stood and pointed to me. "The foster mother is here, Your Honor."

The judge referred to his notes and continued. "We're also addressing a possible violation of Judge Moreno's order that the whereabouts of the foster home and the identities of foster parents were to remain confidential. Is that right?" He directed this query to the county's attorney.

"That's correct, Your Honor. The county had requested this provision, given the disruption of previous foster placements."

The father's attorney, Lynn Cutler, looked up from her notes to protest. "Those facts are in dispute, your Honor." Seeing this woman again, I was struck that she had the pasty, road-worn look of a chronic drug user. I'd recently learned she was not familiar with family law and made her living defending drug dealers.

"You'll get your chance, counselor. Am I to understand the court order has been violated?" The judge was absorbed in his notes, so the attorneys didn't know whom he was addressing.

"If I may, Your Honor." Dave buttoned his suit jacket as he stood again. "We believe the court order has been violated."

The judge continued thumbing through his files and glanced at his watch. "We have a lot of things to cover today, so let's deal with this first. Let's hear from the foster mother."

Dave scooted his chair back so I could get to the witness stand. After I was sworn in, there was a lull in the proceedings. Everyone was busy, whispering, checking notes, fumbling through files; even Timothy Clyde occupied himself with examining his fingernails. Maybe I was worried about nothing, but I was glad Dave had coached me on what to say.

Dave started with the line of questioning we'd practiced, hoping to introduce testimony about the traumatic birth family visits. "Why did you feel it necessary to get the children into therapy, Ms. Marshall?"

"The kids seemed really stressed after visiting with their parents."

Cutler wasn't going to let that go. "Objection. This is outside of Ms. Marshall's expertise." The judge agreed, so Dave rephrased.

"Describe the children's behavior after visiting with Mr. and Mrs. Clyde."

I glanced down at the notebook in my lap where I'd summarized what happened after each visit. As I began to describe how depressed and traumatized the children were, Cutler interrupted again.

"Your Honor, this is not proof the children were distressed after seeing their parents. They may be upset about being separated from them and having to live with these people." I made a point of not looking at her. I wasn't going to give her the satisfaction of knowing she had upset me with this ridiculous statement. I waited for the judge to rule, as I'd been coached.

"I'll allow it. Do we have a report from the therapist?" the judge said.

"We do, Your Honor." Rick held up the document. The children's therapist agreed the visits were causing psychological distress and recommended they be reduced or eliminated.

"I'll read it later. Proceed."

"What happened when you met the birth parents for their visit on September fifteenth?"

"My husband and I were—"

"Objection. This has nothing to do with the determination of the removal of parental rights."

This woman was irritating beyond belief.

"Overruled. I need to remind counsel we are addressing a possible violation of a court order. Proceed."

"As we dropped off the children at the agreed upon meeting place, a woman came up behind me and blocked my car door as I was trying to close it. My first reaction was that I thought we were being robbed."

"Objection, Your Honor. Ms. Marshall's feelings are not evidence for the facts."

"I'll allow it. I would like the foster mother to proceed with describing her experience without interruption."

Rick smiled and Dave nodded for me to go on. I described how the private investigator badgered me for our name and address and threatened us as we drove off. My voice shook as I relayed how scared we were for our safety and the children's welfare. The judge seemed deep in thought as he listened and nodded. When I finished my story, the courtroom was quiet waiting for the judge to speak.

"Ms. Cutler, it appears you defied Judge Moreno's order regarding the anonymity of the foster parents. You will explain to me later why you should not be cited for contempt. Ms. Marshall, you can be seated."

As I walked back to my seat, Timothy Clyde glared at me and then whispered something to his attorney, jingling his shackles as he pointed in my direction.

A supervisor from DSS took the stand next and described how the county had tried to work with the Clydes to help them reunite with their children. It had provided referrals to counselors, parenting classes, housing, and job placement. The Clydes refused counseling, did not complete the parenting classes, and never acquired a steady job or housing for their family. The county had not heard from them for months until recently, when the adoption was ordered.

As I listened to this testimony, I felt as if I were looking out on a desert landscape with the prospect of trudging through deep sand dunes and sinking to my knees with each step. At that time, I had no idea I would sit through twenty more tedious and often absurd court sessions. This case would be the longest in the county's history for removing parental rights, over two and a half years of litigation involving five attorneys, all paid for by Alameda County.

No one counted the cost to our family.

17

THE SHADOW

As Kayla chatted with me about her plans to see a movie, a ghostly image streaked behind her. We continued to talk, but I was distracted by a need to investigate. I was growing accustomed to this sensation: prickliness and a tightening of the skin around my skull. I excused myself and went exploring. Robert sat on his bed, disassembling a toy using a screwdriver from my toolbox.

"What are you doing there?"

"Fixing something."

"I don't remember you asking me if you could borrow my screwdriver. You need to ask next time."

"Okay."

"If you want to fix something, why don't you help Daddy Michael with that sprinkler he's working on."

"Can I use the screwdriver?"

"I think it'll come in handy."

He slid off his bed and hurried to the backyard, where Michael was repairing a sprinkler while Jenny played nearby. Michael looked up at me and frowned as I watched from the patio door. He wasn't happy about the added job of finding something for Robert to do, but he put him to work digging around the broken part. I felt better knowing he was under Michael's watchful eye.

Unlike kids who took things apart out of curiosity, Robert stole dangerous objects like scissors and screwdrivers and used these tools to destroy things. He seemed oddly comforted when we became upset, but our lectures and consequences did nothing to change his behavior. We were growing afraid he would hurt himself, and we found we needed to keep an eye on him more than his younger sister.

I watched them for a minute more and then went into the kitchen to make sandwiches for the next day. We prepared lunches for everyone except Jenny, who was fed at day care and got lots of snacks at preschool. We knew kids often traded their food at school and didn't always eat what we fixed them, but a couple of times this past week, Robert had run out the door without his lunch.

The first time this happened, he yelled over his shoulder, "Not hungry!" and was halfway across the street before I could stop him. I thought he would learn not to skip lunch and that would be the end of it. When he did it again, Michael made a point of handing him his lunch while he dressed for school, but he still left it behind. Later that evening we got a call from his teacher.

"Mrs. Sievert, I have to insist that Robert either bring a lunch or you give him money to buy it at school. If you can't afford to feed him, you can apply for the free lunch program."

"Mrs. Brady, I assure you, we've been providing him lunch."

"Well, that's not what's happening. I had some of the children come to me worried about him. A few have given him their lunches, and I've received one complaint from a parent that his own child went hungry because she gave most of her food to Robert."

"I'm sorry. I did explain to you that he's our foster child and I'm afraid he has some food anxieties." I was embarrassed that Robert's teacher thought we were negligent.

"You did, and I sympathize, but you should know he told me he was scrounging from the others because you don't have time to make him a lunch."

"You know that's not true. We'll talk to him about this. He shouldn't be begging from the other kids. I appreciate your letting me know."

"All right, but be sure to tell him we talked. I don't want him thinking he's pulling the wool over my eyes." As I hung up the phone, I considered why Robert was giving others the impression he wasn't cared for. Was he trying to convince people we were bad parents? We could get in trouble if people believed him. It was possible he was only using these stories to get others to feel sorry for him and give him things.

During the children's weekly visits with Dr. Diana, we updated her about the latest incidents of Robert's lying, stealing, and destruction. She indicated his behaviors could be warning signs he was sociopathic. While I wasn't ready to accept this diagnosis, Michael was very alarmed. "What does this mean? Are we in danger?"

"I think you need to be on the lookout for other signs, such as torturing pets or fire setting," she said. "We've seen recent studies that sociopaths showed early signs in childhood. Stay alert and be consistent with your consequences for these behaviors."

The household took on a jumpy air. Jenny and Kayla were on edge and went to great lengths to hide valuables from Robert's sticky fingers. The thieving became so routine that as soon as anyone noticed something missing, we searched Robert's room. When items I didn't recognize began showing up there, I knew we'd moved into new territory.

After Robert's class went on a field trip to the Oakland Museum, we found several gift shop items that were too expensive for him to buy with his allowance. I showed him the necklace and key chains I had found and asked for an explanation.

"I bought these with my allowance, for you," he said.

"Robert, this necklace still has the price tag on it. It cost thirty dollars. I don't believe you."

"Why don't you ever believe me?"

"Because you've stolen and lied before and you couldn't have bought these with a five-dollar-a-week allowance. You can get in a lot of trouble stealing from stores."

"I didn't take them."

"Robert."

He sat on his bed and hung his head. "Will I have to go to jail like my Dad?"

While I hoped he would take this issue seriously, I was taken aback. Was that what he wanted?

"No, but you have to admit you did this and return the items and apologize."

I called the museum and told them what had happened. I asked if someone would accept our return of the items and talk to my son about the seriousness of stealing. I knew it was a lot to ask, but the museum staff was willing. "We've all been there," the security guard said. "Let me handle it."

The information desk directed us to the basement office of museum security. The uniformed African-American man seated behind the metal desk stood to an intimidating six foot four and motioned us to sit on the folding chairs in front of him. While I sat down, Robert placed the stolen items on his desk. He stood next to me, stiff as a little soldier.

"What do you have to say?" I asked.

"I'm sorry." Robert's voice was barely audible in the stark, windowless room.

"Young man, do you know what happens when we catch someone stealing from the museum?"

Robert shook his head.

"We call the police. Sometimes people are put in handcuffs and jailed. Should I call the police?"

Robert shook his head again and looked at me, clearly worried. I had assured him that wouldn't happen. Was I going to let them take him away?

"Robert, you have to understand how serious this is," I said. "You can't steal from anyone, ever."

Robert nodded. He wore the owl face I'd seen many times before—he looked as lost as I felt. How was I going to help him stop doing this?

The guard continued. "Son, look at me. This is your one and only warning. If you ever steal from the museum again, I'll call the police and they'll take you to juvenile hall. That will not be a picnic." He drove home his point by drilling his finger on the desk. I watched them both, hoping Robert had learned something.

"Do you have anything else to say?" I asked. Robert shook his head *no*.

"All right then."

As we walked out of the office, I turned and mouthed *thank you* to the security guard. He nodded and closed the door behind us.

When we arrived home, Robert went straight to his room as ordered; we had grounded him for a week.

"How did it go at the museum?" Michael asked. "Do you think he learned a lesson?"

"It's hard to tell. He looked nervous when the security guard talked to him. Maybe it'll have some effect."

"I hope he grows out of this. I'm checking into getting a lock for our bedroom, but now I have something to show you. You've got to see what I found today when I checked the sprinklers." We went to the side of the house and he pointed. Irrigation valves lay in pieces with the wiring exposed.

"I'm amazed he didn't get shocked," Michael said. He stood with his hands on his hips, shaking his head as I knelt to examine the damage. How could he have done this without hurting himself? When did he do this?

"I don't know what to say," I said.

"I know. I'll call a plumber to replace the valves and install a lock box over them. I think we're running out of ideas for consequences. We may need to face the reality that we are living with a severely damaged little boy."

Out of the corner of my eye, the blinds moved: Robert watching our reaction as we assessed the damage. I felt discouraged as I picked up my screwdriver from the dust. A broken sprinkler valve can be fixed. Robert needed way more help than Michael and I could give him.

18

JEKYLL AND HYDE

The office was dimly lit and overstuffed with pillows and afghans. Though it was midday, the blinds were closed and covered with heavy drapes. Michael and I sat on a sofa, separated by a large throw pillow. The couple's therapist looked like a college professor in his brown corduroy jacket with elbow patches. He gripped an unlit pipe between his teeth while he took notes. He studied Michael, who'd been speaking for a while about how miserable his life was—or more precisely, how miserable I made his life. Michael was comfortable confiding in a therapist. He'd been to a few, working through childhood issues caused by a mentally ill mother. I was wary about how honest I could be in these sessions, knowing I might have to deal with the repercussions later.

"So, Catherine, Michael said he's pretty unhappy. How are you feeling?"

"A little anxious."

"Why's that?"

"When Michael's unhappy, that usually means he's angry with me. I'm not looking forward to the conversation we'll have later."

Michael glared at me. To strangers, he was charming and erudite, and he could be that way with me as well. But often he was moody and abusive, and I walked on eggshells, never knowing which "Michael" would show up.

"What happens when he's angry with you?"

I pulled the pillow closer, fiddling with the fringe.

"I get the cold shoulder, door slamming, that kind of thing. He yells at me. I've gotten hit a couple of times."

"Michael, care to comment?"

"We've had some shoving matches. She pushes my buttons. She deliberately provokes me ..." Michael started to provide a sampling of my behaviors that caused the problem, but the therapist cut him off.

"It's important everyone feel they can speak freely here. Catherine, tell me what you mean when you say you got hurt."

"A few bruises. He once ..."

Michael interrupted again. "My life is a nightmare. I work at a demanding job and come home to a disaster every day." His complaints continued as the therapist took notes.

When we first met, I had tolerated his artist's temperament, but now I saw it as an excuse to be self-absorbed and chronically unhappy. Of course, our lives were stressful dealing with the three children, but why take it out on me? I never knew from day to day whether he would be the bright, charming man I married or a mean and moody bully. I was living with Jekyll and Hyde.

"Michael, you may benefit from individual sessions before we continue with couple's therapy." The psychologist pulled out his appointment book, and that was my cue to get out the checkbook. I suppressed the feelings of resentment surfacing. This had happened before when we'd tried counseling. After a few minutes of observing Michael, it was evident what the real issue was.

On the way home, Michael slid in a tape of Handel's *Messiah* and sang along. I was glad he was in good spirits for once. Maybe he was pleased he was getting more attention to his needs. I stared out the window at the bare trees and front-yard Christmas decorations, which looked dismal in the daylight. I had tried so hard to marry someone who was not like my father, and here I was walking on eggshells just like I did when I was growing up.

"You know, I think I need to see a therapist too," I said. "It would help me if I had someone to talk to." I hated how I sounded, so needy, as if I were asking his permission to spend money on something frivolous, like dancing lessons.

"You know the county won't pay for this, and we can only afford to have one of us go."

"I know. It would be nice, though. It feels like things are piling up …"

"You know how I can be. I'd hate to imagine what would happen if I don't get help."

The implied threat hung in the air. Who could argue with that? Who would want to?

When we arrived home, the kids greeted us at the door, eager to start the Christmas cookie decorating we'd planned. The day before, Michael and the children had made sugar cookies, pressing the dough into Santas, Christmas trees, and candy canes. While we were at the therapist, Kayla prepared everything else, laying out the kitchen table with the racks of baked cookies, bowls of homemade cream frosting, food coloring, sprinkles, and silver balls. I put one of my aprons around Jenny and lifted her onto her step stool so she could reach.

Michael was good at helping the kids with these holiday projects. He paid attention to the details and encouraged the children to be creative. I took pictures of everyone making a happy mess, Michael and the kids posing with their best cookie designs. They all looked like they were having a good time.

Just like a normal family.

19

KAYLA'S DECISION

Kayla felt she'd made a terrible mistake in coming to live with us. She hadn't made many friends at school, and the bullies continued to bother her on the city bus. She tried to help the kids, but Robert's behaviors were making her nervous. Michael and I fighting didn't help much. She knew she would have to share her room with Jenny soon, and that loss of privacy seemed like the last straw. It was understandable that Kayla complained to her mother about her life here. When Michael overheard her begging to go back to Toronto, he confronted her.

"Why are you doing this?" Michael asked. "Your mother says you call her every week with nothing but complaints. Do you really want to quit school here and go back?"

"You don't want me here. Why do you care? You probably wish I would go so you'd have one less headache." Kayla was sobbing now, her face buried in her hands.

"That's not true, Kayla," I said. "We're happy you're here. You're an important part of this family."

"Why do you keep calling your mother about all these problems in the house? It's none of her business." Michael looked at me for support. "Remember last year, all the calls we got from Kayla about how miserable she was at home?" He turned to Kayla. "Make up your mind. Are you unhappy here or unhappy there. Or are you just unhappy?"

Kayla jumped up and ran out of the room, sobbing. "I hate this place. I want to go home."

Michael and I looked at each other, shocked at her reaction and unclear what we should do next. I'd hoped we'd have a calm discussion, but Michael was embarrassed that his ex-wife knew about some of our problems. His angry reaction fueled Kayla's misery. Her unhappiness had been building up while we were distracted with the children's issues.

Seconds later we heard a crash and the sounds of tinkling glass. We rushed to her room and found her staring at her fists in disbelief. Heaps of shredded safety glass littered her dresser and the carpet.

"Are you all right?" I checked her over to see if she was bleeding. It appeared she'd pounded on her window, and only the blinds had prevented her from being injured. She sat on her bed, in shock. When I moved next to her, she leaned on my shoulder and covered her face in embarrassment. I tried to comfort her. "Look, we'll clean this up and then you need to get some rest. We can talk about this tomorrow."

"I'll get a broom," Michael said. The children stood in the hallway, looking worried, and he scooted them back into their rooms as he passed. "Go back to bed. Kayla had an accident." I tucked the kids back in bed while Michael and Kayla cleaned up the mess and taped cardboard over the broken window.

The next day I suggested to Michael that it might be better if I tried talking to Kayla alone. My relationship with her was different from the one she had with her parents, more like an older sister or an aunt. I felt I had a better chance at helping her think things through, but I needed this discussion to occur outside the house, away from everyone's earshot and Michael's interference. After dinner, I announced that Kayla and I were going for a drive.

"We are?" She looked up at me, surprised. "I have homework," she said.

"We won't be gone long. I just want to talk." We drove out of Livermore, heading east on highway 580. I had a plan. I needed to show Kayla I cared for her, but she had to make a decision so we could keep the drama down.

"Where are we going?" Kayla asked.

"I just want us to be able to talk in private about what you want to do. It might be easier without your dad or the kids around."

"I'm sorry I scared everybody. The window ... I don't know what happened."

"It's okay." We drove in silence for several miles, up out of the valley, winding through the Altamont Pass. It was getting dark earlier, and the evening commute to the Central Valley had died down. We passed slow-moving semis on our right, and late commuters sped by us on our left. I pulled off the highway onto a side road leading to a Park and Ride. There was nothing in the lot but a telephone booth illuminated by a halogen lamp. I parked beside it and turned off the ignition.

"I know adjusting to Robert and Jenny in the house has been hard for you, and it certainly isn't easy coming to a new school for your senior year."

"You told me you were becoming foster parents and I decided to come anyway. I just feel like I made a terrible mistake and I'm stuck."

"Nothing is forever, Kayla. It's just till May. Hang in there till the end of school, and then you can go back. Think of this year as an adventure."

"I don't know. Everything's so hard." She looked out the window. I was glad I would never be seventeen again, but here I was, twenty years older and just as racked with regret and self-doubt. Who was I to advise her? But I had to stay focused. Kayla's indecision was an additional drama we didn't need right now. I reached in the backseat to get my purse.

"This is my long-distance card for the pay phone. If you want to return to Toronto, call your mother now and tell her to buy you a one-way ticket back. Everyone will understand, and no one wants you to be unhappy. If you think you want to stay, you have to promise to stick it out and finish high school here. No more waffling. Decide whether you're in or out, and then let's move on."

Kayla looked at the phone card, then at the phone booth. I settled back in the driver's seat and stared straight ahead, careful to wear a neutral expression. She needed to decide. Moments passed.

"I'll stay."

"You're sure? You can't change your mind anymore. This will be your decision."

"I'll stick it out. I'm sorry."

"I'm glad you said that. I didn't want you to go." I pulled a Kleenex out of the glove box and gave her one. "And I wish things were easier for you. If we only had a magic wand ..."

"Me too." She blew her nose.

"Okay. Let's go home." I pulled out of the parking lot and onto the highway ramp. Kayla chatted on the ride back, something about her chemistry partner and the homework she had to do. I tried to listen, but my mind was on other things. Why couldn't I focus? There were so many problems to solve, and I was growing aware that I only had so much energy to devote to each one. I felt like a robot, checking catastrophes off my list.

20

THE RAP SHEET

The woman on the stand shifted in her seat and glanced nervously at Timothy Clyde and his attorney. She was thin and pale and wore a scarf to cover her hairless head. The testimony of Robert and Jenny's former foster mother was important, but her late-stage cancer had almost kept her from coming to court.

Timothy and Lisa Clyde were with their usual entourage—two attorneys and Timothy's prison escort. Michael and I sat in the gallery section this time since I didn't need to testify. It was important one of us be present for each court session to show the judge how committed we were.

Rick, the children's attorney, thanked her for coming and began his questions. "Mrs. Brockhurst, how long were you and your husband the foster parents for Robert and Jenny Clyde?"

"About nine months."

"You knew the Clydes previously?"

"Yes, we'd been friends. We'd hung out together over the years. They asked us to foster their kids to keep them close by."

"And how did that work out?"

"Not good. Sometimes Lisa and Tim just disappeared for a couple of months, and then the next thing we knew they're on our doorstep demanding to see their kids. No call or nothing."

"Objection." The judge looked up at the source of the interruption, Tim Clyde's attorney. When she didn't supply a reason he asked, "What grounds, counselor?"

"Uh, prejudicial, your honor." She'd jostled Tim's guard when she stood and he backed up his chair to keep from getting stepped on.

"Overruled. Proceed with your account, Mrs. Brockhurst." I liked this judge. He was the same handsome man who had let me tell my story on the stand.

"I understand at one point you had to take the children to the hospital. Can you tell us about that?"

"The Clydes took the kids out to the lake by our house. They kept them out all day, apparently without sun protection. When they returned, Jenny was badly sunburned. She's so fair she got the worst of it. Later in the evening they both started to blister something awful. I took them to the emergency room, where they were treated for dehydration and second-degree burns."

Rick had told me about this episode, but hearing it again made my stomach turn. How could anybody be that stupid?

"It sounds like you did the right thing. What happened next?"

"I had to report it. I got that foster care license and was paid by the county to take care of the kids. I didn't want to get into trouble or have anyone blame us. Besides, the hospital reported it too."

"Then what happened?"

"Well, the Clydes didn't like it. They came back to the house, stood on the front porch, and yelled at us in front of our neighbors. They were mad because the lady from DSS said they'd had enough chances and the kids needed to be adopted. They said they were going to lose their kids and it was all our fault."

"Was that the end of it?"

"No. We had a lot of bad stuff happen then. Our tires were slashed. Someone came to my husband's work and told lies about him, nearly got him fired. When our trash cans caught on fire, we knew we had to stop being foster parents for Robert and Jenny. It was a shame, too, because I had just found a special preschool for Jenny to help her learn to talk."

"This was about a year ago, is that right?"

"Yeah. I found out I was sick anyway. I would've had to give them up after all."

"Thank you for your testimony today. I appreciate you making the drive when you weren't feeling well."

"Ms. Cutler, did you have questions for the witness?" the judge asked.

"A few, thank you, Your Honor.

"How did you and the Clydes meet?" she asked.

"Beg your pardon?"

"Where did your husband and Timothy Clyde first become friends?"

"Oh, I see. Tim Clyde was still serving time for manslaughter of the sheriff's wife in that traffic accident and ..."

"Your husband was serving time with him, right?"

Rick broke in. "I believe Mrs. Brockhurst was answering the question. Objection—counsel is testifying." It was a point for us that the court records now included mention of this earlier felony.

"Yes, Barry served his time for dealing. That's all behind us."

"Isn't it true that your husband was dealing drugs while he was a foster parent?" Cutler continued.

"No, it is not. That's the lie that was told to his boss and nearly got him fired. Tim Clyde is the drug dealer. Everybody knows that. My husband is out of the business, like I said." She looked very weak and about ready to faint. The drive from the Central Valley, the testimony, and this attack were taking a toll.

Rick came to her defense. "Your honor, I strongly object. The issue is not whether Mr. and Mrs. Brockhurst were good foster parents. We're here to determine the suitability of the Clydes. This is all a distraction."

"I agree. Sustained. Counsel, do you have any questions about this witness's testimony?"

"Your honor, the fact that Mr. and Mrs. Brockhurst were unsuitable also indicates they used poor judgment and overreacted by taking the children to the hospital. This action jeopardized my clients' chances to be reunited with their children."

I scribbled the comment *what a crock* in my notebook and poked Michael to look. The running theme in these court sessions was that the Clydes were the victims of an unfair system. I had no sympathy for these deadbeats.

"I've ruled," the judge said. "The Brockhursts acted in the best interests of the children by reporting the incident to the county. If they'd overreacted, the emergency room wouldn't have treated the children or reported the neglect to Children's Protective Services. Let's excuse the witness. Thank you."

Everyone watched as a friend helped the poor woman out of the witness chair. As she passed by the gallery, I whispered *thank you*. She stopped to speak to us. "I want those children to have a chance." It had been brave of her to come. I learned she died a few months later.

The judge called a lunch recess. Michael and I joined David and Rick at the plaintiff table. The county's attorney continued to make notes and didn't look up. She'd not been involved with any of our strategy sessions and was focused on making sure DSS was not going to be held liable. As foster parents, we did not warrant her protection or her attention.

"I have a surprise." Rick positioned himself so the opposite table wouldn't see and wiggled his eyebrows like Groucho Marx.

"What's up?" Michael asked. Dave rolled his eyes at Rick's theatrics.

"We're introducing Timothy Clyde's rap sheet." Rick pointed to the two-inch thick computer printout. "It's rather extensive."

"What would this prove? It's obvious he's in jail now." Michael said.

"If Timothy Clyde can't stay out of jail, it's pretty clear he's not going to be able to provide for his family," Dave said. "We're playing hardball."

After lunch, the judge allowed the attorney for Timothy Clyde to chronicle how DSS had failed to help the Clydes reunify with their children. The county's attorney presented her account of the numerous attempts to help them. This routine was getting old.

It was Rick's turn to speak. "Your honor, the issue at hand is whether the Clydes have made sufficient progress to support a reunification plan. While we want to acknowledge Mrs. Clyde completed a parenting class and attempted to find work a year ago, most of the county's basic requirements have not been met. Much of this is due to Mr. Clyde's repeated incarcerations and refusal to cooperate. I have here his criminal record …" Rick stepped away from the table, holding the top of the rap sheet, allowing the two-inch-thick pile of continuous feed computer paper to drop to the floor. "This extensive criminal record begins over ten years ago when Timothy Clyde was convicted of vehicular manslaughter. Shall I enter into the record the subsequent convictions for assault, drug possession, drug sales, parole violations, and the domestic violence charge that resulted in the children being removed from the home by Children's Protective Services?"

Mr. Clyde's attorney was on her feet, sputtering with indignation. Timothy Clyde smirked. He looked proud, like someone had just read his résumé.

"I don't think we need a reading of the entire record, Mr. Sanchez," the judge said. The visual of Clyde's criminal record in piles on the floor had its intended effect. It was clear Tim Clyde was not going to be able to stay out of jail long enough to support his children.

"Your honor, if I may." The skinny kid appointed as Mrs. Clyde's attorney spoke for the first time. "We would like to proceed with the reunification plan for Mrs. Clyde alone." I hoped no one heard me groan.

"All right, then. Let's set a date," the judge said. "Mrs. Clyde, for this court to consider reunification, you will need to have a job and an appropriate place for the children to live. I'll give you ninety days and I expect to see significant progress. Is that understood?" Lisa Clyde looked like she'd awakened from a nap. She bobbed her head on cue from her attorney.

"The clerk will work with the attorneys to schedule the next hearing. That's all for today." The judge stood and walked out of the courtroom before everyone could get to their feet.

Across the street from the courthouse, Michael, Steve, Rick, and I sat in what was now our regular booth and ordered drinks: scotches for the guys and a rum and Coke for me.

"I feel like I'm stuck in a nightmare," I said. No one seemed to notice. Rick and Dave were busy congratulating each other on the points they'd scored. Michael was caught up in their enthusiasm and seemed fascinated by the courtroom strategy. The three replayed the hearing highlights like postgame commentators.

I studied my drink and took a long sip. There was still so much that could go wrong.

21

The Easter Moose

See, Mommy?" Jenny was so proud of her Easter egg, dipped in pink dye and covered in glitter. "Oh, nice job, Honey. Tell me, whatcha got there?" I could see she'd drawn a face on the egg, but I needed a clue.

"It's a bunny," Robert said.

"Let's let Jenny tell us, okay?"

"A bunny," she said. She climbed back onto her step stool at the kitchen table, tangling herself in the apron she wore.

Robert and Michael sat side by side, intent on their works of art. Michael cut tiny hats and bunny ears out of construction paper while Robert drew designs on his eggs with the precision of an engineer.

I pulled out my camera to capture the moment. "Say, Happy Easter," I said. Everyone humored me by holding up their creations and flashing smiles.

It was my job to document holidays and birthdays. These Easter photos would go next to the ones we took at Thanksgiving with all of us seated around a hefty turkey dinner. The captions rarely described what was really going on. Everyone had been so grumpy and unhelpful last Thanksgiving that I almost left the house in a huff.

Christmas morning was a little better, but not much. Our modest gifts for the children of books, clothes, and art supplies were overshadowed by gaudy, expensive presents from the birth parents. They gave Jenny a Barbie and a white winter parka trimmed in rabbit fur, and Robert got a remote-control monster car that needed six D batteries. It made a revving noise that set my teeth on edge. I did not waste time worrying about whether these items might get lost or broken, and once the holiday was over, the gifts were buried at the backs of the kids' closets.

Robert hopped off his chair when the kitchen timer went off. I had promised he could test the doneness of the white cake with a toothpick. We were making a special Easter cake and he had asked to be in charge. After getting his go-ahead, I pulled the rounds out of the oven and placed them on racks to cool. He wanted to mix the icing, but egg decorating was more interesting. Left on my own, I dumped a box of powdered sugar into a mixing bowl and stirred in a half a cup of margarine and a capful of imitation vanilla extract. Some of the sugar spilled out on the counter when I stirred, so I transferred the concoction to a larger bowl, scooping in the pile before anybody noticed. I set out the icing, coconut, and jelly beans so the kids could put on the finishing touches when they were finished with the eggs.

We were making an Easter bunny cake like my mother made when I was a kid. I stared at the two round pans of white cake and tried to recall what came next. My mother had a knack for arts and crafts, but I had not inherited this skill. I knew the original directions for the bunny cake came from a women's magazine, probably *Redbook* or *Good Housekeeping*, and the page was folded in Mom's recipe box in Wichita. *This can't be that hard*, I thought. I pulled out some scratch paper and drew two circles. One round had to be the face. I needed ears for sure. I'd cut those from the second cake round. What should I do with the leftover? Was that the body? The shape that remained after I drew the ears did not look anything like a bunny body.

"Guys, I'll be right back. I have to call Grandma." Since I wasn't willing to admit to anyone that I didn't know how to make a bunny cake, I headed off to the privacy of our bedroom.

"Okay." Robert said. Jenny started to follow me. "Honey, go finish your Easter eggs with Daddy."

"Wanna talk to Grandma." Jenny had never met Grandma, but loved to chat on the phone now that she was learning a few new words. "Okay, just say 'hi' and then go back and help Daddy." Jenny said her hellos and ran back to the kitchen. Once she was out of earshot I got down to business.

"Mom, how did you make that Easter bunny cake? I've made the white cake and butter icing, and have the coconut and jelly beans. How do you cut the cake?"

"I haven't made that for years. One round is the face. You made the cake in rounds, right?"

"I got that part …"

"Give me a minute … You just cut the ears out of the second cake and use the rest for the tie."

"What tie?"

"The Easter Bunny wears a bow tie."

"What about the body?"

"There's no body. What do you need a body for?

"Okay. I'll figure it out. Thanks, Mom. How are you and Dad doing?"

I had learned a long time ago that my mother and I had different ways of communicating and there was nothing to be gained by being impatient. For Mom, recipes were a dash of this and a handful of that, while I preferred precise directions.

When I returned to the kitchen, Robert and Jenny were ready to make the Easter bunny cake. Since the kitchen table was full of decorated eggs, they pulled their chairs up to the counter. I covered a large cookie sheet with foil, slid a knife around one of the cake rounds, and plopped it onto the sheet. It landed in one piece. Within the second cake, I carved out two ear shapes. Using spatulas, I lifted them from the rest of the cake and gingerly placed them on the cookie sheet above what was going to be the head. The ears, carved in the curve of the pan, pointed inward like a devil's horns. *This couldn't be right.* I used the spatulas and switched them around. Robert frowned as he watched me rearrange the pieces and then looked at me like I'd lost my mind. Jenny peered around me, squealed, and pointed. "Oooh, a moose," she said.

She was right. Our Easter bunny ears looked more like antlers. *Close enough.* We slathered on the white icing, sprinkled on coconut, and added jelly beans for the eyes, nose, and mouth. Michael took our picture while I tilted the cake and the kids pointed and smiled. Thanks to Jenny, we had a caption for our photo: *The Easter Moose.* There was a section of the cake left over, so we covered it with icing and coconut and ate it as a snack, polishing off the extra jelly beans. I'm sure our Easter bunny cake did not resemble the one in the women's magazine, but it was good enough for us.

A recipe for the Easter bunny cake,
typed and drawn by my mother, is on page 188.

22

WHO KNEW?

What are you doing, Jenny?" I asked. My daughter held a baby doll tucked under one arm while she talked on a play phone and tried not to drop my old briefcase.

"Playing mommy," she said.

"Playing mommy? You look pretty busy."

"I'm a busy mommy."

"I see. Would you get your brother so we can fold laundry?"

"Okay." She ran off, bellowing Robert's name and dropping her baby in the hall. *Oops.* Losing the baby was not a good sign. Maybe I wasn't such a good role model after all.

Robert poked his head out of his room. "Mommy wants you," Jenny said.

Robert clamped his hands over his ears. "You don't have to yell."

I intervened before they got into an argument. "Robert, we need to get the clothes out of the dryer, fold them, and put them away. Jenny can help. You want to go swimming this afternoon, right?" Our social worker had thought it'd be a good idea if we met other foster-adopt families, and we were surprised to learn there was one in our neighborhood. We had an invitation to swim at their pool.

Robert scuffed his shoes along the carpet as he followed me out to the garage. Like most kids, he didn't like doing chores, especially ones he called "girls' work."

We carried baskets of dried clothes to the family room, dumped them on the sofa, and organized them into piles. I reminded Jenny how to fold her shirts and pants, and then left them to it. I had some things to finish at my desk, so I set the timer for thirty minutes, a strategy I was experimenting with so I could work at home without interruption. After a few minutes I heard Robert murmuring something to Jenny.

"I know how to do it, Robert. Leave me alone." Loud and firm, my little girl was not taking any guff from her big brother.

The house grew quiet as the children got to work. I missed my step-daughter, Kayla, who was back in Toronto after graduating from Livermore High in June. The house was not the same without her. After some time, I became aware that the children were hovering nearby, hoping I noticed they'd finished their chore.

"Mom," Robert said.

"I didn't hear the timer go off yet," I said.

"I know, but we want to get ready for swimming. Do we change here or take our swimming suits with us?"

"Go ahead and change. I'll be finished in a minute. I want to see all your clothes put away nicely." Robert let out a whoop, and they raced down the hall to get ready.

The walk to the home of the other foster-adopt family was slow going with the kids in their flip-flops and our armloads of snacks and water toys. Their place was the same model as ours, but instead of a patchy lawn and weeds in back, they had a swimming pool surrounded by a concrete terrace, landscaping, and expensive pool furniture.

"It was nice of you to invite us, Sara," I said. "We didn't know you were so close by or we'd have gotten together sooner."

Younger than me by about ten years, she was dressed in a crisply ironed shirt and shorts outfit. Her makeup didn't mask the dark circles under eyes. "I'm glad we could manage it. We have to stick together, if only to compare notes." She smiled and then we both turned our attention to the children.

My kids slipped into the pool and inched toward the little girl in a yellow bathing suit standing in the middle of the shallow end. Charlotte had dark curly hair and droopy brown eyes and looked big for a five-year-old.

Sara leaned over the edge and coaxed her daughter. "Charlotte, why don't you show Robert and Jenny how to play Marco Polo?" Charlotte stared at my kids, then stuck her thumb in her mouth.

"Robert, share your toys. Maybe Charlotte wants to play with them," I said. Charlotte turned away and splashed over to her own toys by the side of the pool.

Sara and I gave up and headed for a shaded table. She slumped into her chair and poured me a glass of iced tea. "I'm afraid Charlotte had another bad night," she said. "She throws terrible tantrums, and we can't seem to get her to sleep through the night. We were up till two."

"I'm sorry. We could have rescheduled. You must be exhausted."

"That's all right. I need the company. We finally got her down, but we had to get up again at six. Mark works at the lab." She was referring to the Lawrence Livermore National Laboratory, a major local employer.

"Is she seeing someone for the tantrums? Both of my kids are in therapy." I was hoping if I told her my troubles, she'd share hers and we could commiserate.

Sara leaned close and whispered, holding her tea glass up to her lips. "Her social worker said she was sexually molested. We didn't find out how bad it was until we got her in therapy. We started her on medication, but she's not getting better."

I kept my expression neutral so the children wouldn't see how alarmed I was. "How are you managing?"

"Not very well. Charlotte has destroyed her room. She goes on rampages, and I've been injured trying to keep her from hurting herself. The worst thing is one of the neighbor kids complained Charlotte molested her. We can't let her play with other children unsupervised. We're considering giving her up. We don't have the energy or the resources to give her the help she needs."

I glanced over at Jenny and Robert, relieved they weren't playing with Charlotte. I didn't know what to say to this woman. I had come here hoping for advice, only to discover these foster-adopt parents were worse off than we were. I munched on a cookie and kept my eye on the kids.

"You know, I figured out this foster-adopt racket," she said.

"What do you mean, racket?"

"All the kids in that foster-adopt program are the hardest to place, kids who've been abused or have disabilities or difficult birth parents who're still in the picture."

"That's us." I said.

"See? I talked with other parents and they have kids or situations nobody in their right mind would take."

"Did we make a mistake by going through Social Services?" I asked.

"Not necessarily. I found out from one of the other parents that if you really want to adopt, you should sign up to be a regular foster parent and then take in kids till you get one you want to keep. A lot of foster children haven't been through the mill as much as ours have. If you catch them when they're new in the system, there's a chance they're better candidates for adoption."

I nodded, trying to be polite. I was embarrassed and sad for this woman. Though this approach sounded practical, it felt so wrong. Our kids weren't pets to take back to the pound if it didn't work out. But Louise, our first social worker, had downplayed our children's situation to the point of deception. Would we have decided to adopt these kids if we'd known then what we knew now?

I walked my soggy kids back home, listening to their chatter and pondering what I'd learned. Our children seemed so normal compared to poor Charlotte. I couldn't imagine giving them up, but I couldn't help feeling like we'd been duped. It was as if we'd been invited to play a game, but hadn't been told the rules until it was too late.

23

SEALING THE DEAL

The room went silent. Everyone at our side of the table looked stunned. Had we heard right? For over two years we'd listened to Lisa Clyde complain about how the system was against her and she needed more time. I was sick of her whining and excuses, and I was frustrated that the county acquiesced to her threats of litigation. But the family court system had said *enough* and sent the case to arbitration. After the mediator indicated he was losing patience, Mrs. Clyde's attorney conferred with his client, then stood.

"Mrs. Clyde agrees to waive her parental rights if she is allowed certain conditions that provide her access to the children."

Michael and I tried not to react, but it was difficult. He squeezed my hand under the table—it would have been in bad taste to appear jubilant. Should we hope we were close to the end of this ordeal? Did this mean that after twenty-one family court sessions we were free from this legal limbo and could adopt our children?

Lisa Clyde pulled out a Kleenex as her attorney sat down. Did this capitulation mean she was worn down by the process, or did she have the children's best interests at heart? The biblical scene of Solomon, holding a baby in one hand and sword in the other, pricked my conscience. This couldn't have been easy for her. Yet, I'd always thought stamina would be the deciding factor. I wasn't going to give up and she knew it.

There were details to work out, but the mediator asked for a short break. After more than two years of ongoing court-ordered contact with the birth mother, the children's therapists thought it would be too traumatic for them to never see their birth parents again. I hoped Lisa Clyde would be reasonable. As I left to use the restroom and get a snack, she huddled with her attorney to draw up her demands.

It was near lunchtime and I needed something crunchy to ease my tension. Understanding we had fifteen minutes, I took my time at the snack machine. In the hall, Dave, our attorney, searched for me. "They've started the negotiations, and Michael told them he thought it was okay to let her have monthly visits with the kids. Shall we go with that?"

"What? No! We're coming off of every-other-week visits. I want to cut back to once a quarter at most."

"Well, she also wants longer holiday visits, as well as access to the children's therapists and teachers to track how they're doing."

"Are you kidding me? We're raising these kids, not her." I was looking forward to leaving the foster care system behind, along with all the reporting and supervision. The last thing I wanted was to have Lisa Clyde looking over our shoulder and demanding updates.

Everyone turned as Dave and I entered the courtroom. I shook my head as I walked toward Michael and the children's attorney, making it clear I was not falling in line.

"I think we got it worked out," Michael said. "Once a month visits sounded okay, better than what we have now, right?" He was oblivious to my reaction and looked pleased with himself. He really thought he was helping. I chose my words carefully because I didn't want to embarrass him and have to deal with it later.

"Michael, you remember we talked about this. Quarterly visits are reasonable and that's what we planned to offer. This is our chance to get out from under all these requirements. We definitely cannot have Lisa Clyde involved in the children's school or keeping tabs on their therapy."

"Well, I did the best I could. You were gone and the arbitrator pushed us to wrap up. Let's let this go and be done with it."

Dave was quiet until we looked to him for advice. "Let me counter with the quarterly visits," he said. "If you want to be firm on the other issues you'll have to give on the visitation." I sat next to Michael and said nothing while Dave negotiated for us. I was annoyed with my husband, yet I should have known better than to leave him alone with this. I'd thought we were on the same page, but the pressure was getting to him.

In the end, we agreed to visits with the birth family once every other month. Timothy Clyde could come if he was out of jail and compliant with parole requirements. The arbitrator and social services shot down the idea of letting the birth parents contact the children's teachers and therapists. Mrs. Clyde's attorney comforted her as she sobbed into his shoulder.

Michael and I were exhausted. We had won, but we didn't feel like celebrating.

❖

It was a mild spring day in Hayward; a Tuesday, midday. Those who had court business were inside. No one was around to help us take photos, so Michael and I took turns posing with the children next to the sign for the Alameda County Courthouse. All of us were dressed for the occasion, Michael in his light-blue sport jacket, me in a bright red business suit and matching scarf, and the kids in their Easter outfits. The children held stuffed animals the judge had given them. He was a kind man who relished his role officiating adoptions. Our children answered his questions politely, and Robert shook his hand at the end of the proceedings. Later that day, we celebrated at our favorite Mexican restaurant, like we did on other special occasions.

Robert and Jenny never understood what we went through to get to that day. The struggles with the foster care system, social services, the birth family, and their attorneys and the dreary court hearings were at an end, we hoped. Years later, Michael and I recalled that adoption day with irony. April 2, 1991, almost three years from when our children first came to live with us, just missed being April Fool's Day.

24

GIRLY GIRL

Jenny sat on her bedroom floor changing her dolly's dress, surrounded by a nest of school papers, crayons and markers, dirty clothes, and toys. Her room smelled of the past week's snacks and dirty dishes hidden under her bed. It was Saturday morning cleanup time, but finding Barbie's perfect outfit in the heap proved too much of a distraction.

I stood in her doorway holding the timer that had just dinged. "Jenny, remember what you're supposed to be doing?"

She looked up at me, dazzled by the dolly dress Grandma had made for her. She must have rediscovered it in the pile by her bed. "See, Mommy?"

"Lovely. Now what is it we say when we have a chore to do?"

She scrambled to her feet and we recited a ditty using hand movements: *"First we work and then we can play."* Her teacher had suggested this method as a cue to help Jenny stay focused. We had recently found out our little girl had no capacity for auditory learning. If she heard something, she forgot it. Her teachers had the training and the tools to work with this limitation, but we struggled at home.

"Don't you want to go to dance class? We have to be there by ten—that's only sixty minutes away."

Her eyes widened at the horrible thought of missing her dancing lesson. The hook was set. "Okay, I'm going to set the timer for twenty minutes again. How about you try to finish three things? Beat the timer and you'll get a treat. Get on your mark, get set, go." I reset the timer and went back to the kitchen to finish washing the floor. Her bedroom cleanup would go faster if I helped, but that wouldn't teach her anything. I suspected Jenny was wilier than everyone thought, and it was a challenge to keep one step ahead of her. She had a remarkable talent in getting others to do things for her.

The dance studio, located in a strip mall in north Livermore, was run by a perky, petite woman with a booming voice. Every year each of her classes performed a dance routine during the Fourth of July parade. For Jenny's group, her dance teacher selected a jazzy number from *Cabaret* with too much butt wagging for my taste. Earlier, I had complained to the teacher that I wasn't too pleased with the suggestive moves, but she assured me that no one else complained and, besides, they were just little girls. After the parade, I planned to take Jenny out of dance class and try to interest her in something like karate. I smiled and waved as Jenny stumbled through the routine, mimicking the other girls because she couldn't remember the instructions.

After dance class, we crossed the street for an ice cream. I'd promised her the treat as a reward for cleaning her room. Though she wasn't finished with the chore, I wanted ice cream myself, so we went anyway. Jenny was tall for her age, almost to my shoulders, so she looked older than she was. While we stood in line, she held my hand and leaned against me as I read the flavors I thought she might like. We could struggle through the reading exercise of sounding out the choices, but she was tired from dancing and it would take too long. I ordered bubble gum ice cream in a sugar cone for her and German chocolate ice cream in a cup for me. We ate at a small table and chatted about Girl Scouts.

"Next week we're going to learn how to put on makeup," she said.

"Makeup, at the Girl Scout meeting?"

"Sure. Mrs. Whitaker's daughter sells Mary Kay, so she's going to demonstrate how to put on lipstick and mascara and everything. Everybody gets a sample to take home."

"Honey, you girls are too young for makeup. I thought you were learning camping skills."

"That was Mrs. Jeffreys. She moved away. Mrs. Whitaker says she doesn't like to get dirty, so we're going to be doing inside stuff."

I was dismayed, but Jenny seemed excited about the makeup session, so I dropped it. I had thought Girl Scouts would toughen her up, balance out her girly-ness. I had fond memories of my scouting years, lashing furniture from tree limbs, digging latrines, and cooking over an open fire. Maybe girls didn't do that anymore.

When we returned home, Jenny went back to her room to finish cleaning while I went to my desk to work on some files. After about an hour, she twirled up to me wearing one of my old outfits from the dress-up box, pulled me into her room, and said *tada* with a flourish.

"Good job," I said. At least the carpet was clear so I could vacuum. She pirouetted into the family room to watch TV as her reward. I bent over to plug in the vacuum and noticed papers peeking out from under her bed. Down on all fours, I lifted the dust ruffle and saw most of what had been on floor earlier, now shoveled underneath. I scooped out the trash and clothes and hollered for Jenny to turn off the TV and come back. Score one for Jenny. She had succeeded in getting me to help her after all.

Later that night, I peeked in on both the kids to make sure they were asleep. Robert was tired from Little League and had gone to bed early. When I opened the door to Jenny's room, she was sitting up, chatting with her stuffed animals and dolls. "Honey, you and your babies need to go to sleep."

She stroked the hair of the doll she cradled. "Tabitha's scared."

"You hear the funny voices again?" I asked. She nodded. The past few weeks, Jenny hadn't been able to sleep well because she heard voices, mean ones that scared her. At first I thought she was having nightmares like a lot of kids do at that age, but Dr. Diana thought these hallucinations, along with the learning disabilities, could be a warning sign of something worse. Michael and I had recently learned the extent of mental illness in Jenny's birth family. Early-onset schizophrenia was too frightening a diagnosis to comprehend. I chose instead to focus on helping Jenny feel comfortable enough to sleep.

"I'll make you some cocoa and keep you company till you feel sleepy. If the voices come back, tell them they have to listen to me sing Girl Scout songs. That oughta scare 'em." She giggled.

When I returned with the cocoa, she'd conked out. I tried not to disturb her as I pulled up the covers. Jenny lay in a tangle of dress-up clothes, crayons, and coloring books. A small round mirror lay close to her hand, and when I bent to kiss her good night, I took care not to smear her makeup, rosy cheeks and lips courtesy of the Crayola Company.

25

THE APPRENTICE

Mrs. Sievert? Barbara Collins from Croce Elementary. I'm afraid you need to come to the office right away. Jenny's been suspended for bringing a weapon to school."

"Jenny? A weapon?"

"I know. Hard to believe. She's in the office now. When you come in, she can explain how she got the box cutter. I'm sorry. This means a three-day suspension."

"I'll be right there." How could my sweet eight-year-old daughter come to possess a box cutter? Did she take one of Michael's tools for matting his artwork? The district had strict rules about bringing dangerous things to school, and Robert had already gotten in trouble for a screwdriver in his backpack. I worked my way through lunchtime traffic and worried this might be a sign Jenny was following in Robert's footsteps.

Jenny sat in a plastic chair in the office, occupying herself by swinging her legs and staring at the ceiling. When she saw me, she stopped. I gave her a look that said, *I'll deal with you later,* walked to the counter, and asked for Mrs. Collins. I had paperwork to sign, acknowledging the cause of the suspension. As I took my copy, Ms. Collins handed over the offending item and wished me luck. "I couldn't get much out of her except that she and her brother got them at Safeway."

So Robert had one too, probably stolen, but when had that happened? I thanked her and motioned for Jenny to follow me out to the

113

car. Jenny climbed in and put on her seat belt. I sat in the back beside her and closed the door. "Now, explain. Where did you get the box cutter?"

"At the grocery store."

"You bought box cutters at the grocery store?"

She shook her head.

"You stole them?" She nodded, examining the hem of her sweater.

"Look at me. Tell the truth. When did you go to the grocery store? You know Robert doesn't go to stores without one of us with him."

"We went after Daddy dropped us off at the library."

"When?"

"Last Saturday."

That past weekend, Michael had the kids while I taught a workshop. I recalled he mentioned a plan to meet friends for coffee, and I assumed he took the kids with him. He must have dropped them off at the library and Robert used the opportunity to skip out and rip off another store.

"Mom?"

"Yes."

"Robert said not to tell. I think he's going to be mad."

"You should be worried about whether Daddy and I are mad. You are grounded and that includes no TV for two weeks and lots of weed pulling. You also owe your teacher an apology, but we'll deal with that later."

"Robert better be grounded, too." I gave her another look as I climbed into the driver's seat.

When we arrived home, I raided Robert's room and found a box cutter and a couple of cigarette lighters. Michael and I knew all of his regular hiding places: under his mattress, in his chest of drawers, or in the corner of his closet. We had our routine. Robert stole, he hid the items where he knew we could find them, and we levied some consequence that made no difference. It was like a sad movie replayed in an endless loop.

By the time Michael got home, I'd already grounded Robert and sent him to his room.

"I just wanted a little time with my friends," Michael said. "It's ridiculous we can't trust a twelve-year-old boy to stay in a library with his little sister for an hour or so."

"I know it's ridiculous, but we've learned our lesson. He waits for any time we're off guard. It's like a game to him. Remember the time we left the kids alone at home so we could go to dinner? He hurt himself on purpose, banging his head on the floor till he was bruised. Now he's teaching Jenny his tricks for stealing. One of us has got to be with him all the time."

Michael smacked the wall as he stormed out of the room. A bad mood was in the works. This incident made him look negligent, and he didn't appreciate a lecture from me.

Later that week we drove to Berkeley for the children's therapy appointment. This psychologist was the fourth in six years. The others had either moved on or recommended us to colleagues because they weren't making any progress, particularly with Robert. It was difficult to find child therapists who had experience with foster children, met in the evening, and fit our budget. This office was similar to ones we'd been in before, a waiting room full of indestructible furniture and a kid's corner.

Michael and I met with the therapist first in her office while the children played in the waiting room. We told her about the week's events, and then it was Jenny's turn. After our daughter's session, the therapist called us back in. "I'm afraid we've got a problem," she said. "Jenny told me Robert threatened her. He said he would break her neck if she told the things they've been doing."

"What things?" Michael asked.

"Well, the stealing for one. He's also been teaching her how to smoke. She's been going along with him, but she got caught with the box cutter and she's worried Robert's going to hurt her for telling. I'm required to report this to CPS, you know."

"We're not going to get into trouble for this, are we?" Michael asked, saying aloud what we both feared and had discussed at length. We'd been worrying Robert might harm himself; now there were Jenny and other children to consider. We could be held liable if we didn't do everything we could to protect him and others around him.

She said, "I'm afraid we have to get serious about finding a children's residential center for him. He needs twenty-four-hour supervision and more psychiatric care than I can give him in these weekly visits. Until that happens, you must ensure he doesn't harm Jenny or threaten her further. If he does, you'll have to call the police—and they'll send him to a juvenile detention facility."

Michael groaned. "I don't know what else we can do. I feel like a prison guard as it is."

I took her referral list of children's centers. "This can't be cheap," I said.

"I know. Most of these run between four and five thousand a month. Talk to your worker. The county should pay for this. In the meantime, hang in there. I know you're doing your best."

When we opened the door to the waiting room, we were relieved to see the kids playing quietly in the corner. Robert jumped up and dashed past us, eager to start his session. Michael sat next to Jenny and helped her read a book she'd picked out while I flipped through a dog-eared issue of *Parents Magazine*. We looked up when we heard a crash from the next room, and then Michael pointed at the magazine. "You think you'll find any good ideas in there?"

"Very funny," I said.

26

Narrowing Options

Robert sat cornered in the backseat of our minivan, gripping the door handle as if he were afraid he'd float away. I sat close by, ready to grab him if he tried to jump out. The heavy commute traffic on North 680 impeded our progress, but Michael somehow wove through the stalled lanes, looking back at us in the rearview mirror.

Robert sobbed, indignant and misunderstood; he was just goofing around. I nodded, keeping my arm around his shoulder. There was no point in lecturing him. The situation was out of our hands. The staff of his after-school program had placed a 911 call when they caught him chasing little girls around the playground, flinging lit matches, and threatening to set their hair on fire. When I explained Robert's background to the police, they were sympathetic and gave us two options; either take him to a hospital and "5150" him, a seventy-two-hour psychiatric hold and evaluation, or they'd arrest him and take him to Alameda County Juvenile Hall. Emergency calls to Robert's therapist and social worker cleared the way for admitting him to the children's psychiatric ward of a Walnut Creek hospital.

We parked the car and walked to the lobby with Robert between us, quiet and stoic. The volunteers at the information desk directed us through a maze of elevators and halls to the psychiatric wing. The waiting room was small and brightly lit. A woman in pink scrubs sat behind a sliding glass window, typing on medical forms. She smiled, slid open the glass as we approached, and handed me a clipboard. "Mrs. Sievert?"

I nodded. "Were you the one I spoke to on the phone?" I asked.

"Take a seat till the nurse comes out. She'll be giving your son a physical as part of the admission process. Complete those forms and sign at the bottom."

I felt like I was walking in a fog, following directions without any idea where I was going. Go there, turn here, fill out this form. I looked over at Michael, but he stared straight ahead, lost in his own thoughts.

The three of us sat across the room from the only other occupants: a couple, younger than us, huddled together whispering. I overheard the woman worrying about their daughter, the money, and the options they had left. Her husband reassured her while she dabbed her eyes with a balled-up Kleenex.

A plump woman in identical pink scrubs entered the waiting room and led Robert away. We had no clue what would happen next.

"Are they really going to keep him for seventy-two hours?" I asked.

Michael shrugged, then rose to retrieve a brochure from the counter. "I haven't the slightest idea," he said.

"Maybe one of us should go back home and get his pajamas," I said.

Michael thumbed through the brochure for answers. "Is Janice okay with keeping Jenny all night?" he asked. "They haven't said how long we're supposed to stay here." Jenny's day care provider from years ago had become a friend and had offered to keep Jenny overnight while we sorted out this situation.

The couple noticed our confusion. "They'll come out in a while and tell you to go home," the man said. "You can bring things tomorrow during visiting hours."

"They supply everything, including hospital pajamas," his wife said.

"Thanks. You have a child here?" I didn't want them to know I'd eavesdropped.

"Our daughter. She's twelve. This is the third time we've had to bring her here."

"Oh, so sorry," I said. I couldn't imagine having to do this more than once.

"Yeah, well, it's been a long road," the man said. "She took a fall on her bike two years ago. We thought it was just a concussion, but it caused some other damage, no one's sure what. She hasn't been the same since. She gets violent. Broke Ruth's arm last year."

I didn't know what to say. I was chilled by the idea of being afraid of your own child. We didn't think Robert would ever hurt us on purpose, but we worried about his dangerous behaviors causing accidents.

The woman rubbed her forearm. "We had her in a children's residential treatment facility for about nine months and they stabilized her, but we ran out of money."

"We had to sell our home to pay for it," he said. "We were hoping she'd be better after she was discharged, but she went on a rampage yesterday and busted up some furniture. We locked ourselves in our bedroom till the police came."

"What are you going to do?" My need to know how other families coped overrode my good manners.

"The only option we have left." The man looked at his wife as she reached for another Kleenex from the coffee table. "We're going to give her up so she becomes a ward of the county."

"I don't understand. How does that help?" Michael said.

"How can you do that?" I said. I realized too late my reaction was judgmental. Having worked so hard to adopt Jenny and Robert, I couldn't imagine giving up parental rights voluntarily. But I knew what they were doing even before he explained. This would allow their daughter access to county mental health services they could no longer afford to pay. If they didn't do this, the family would need to become destitute to qualify for services. They were trying to save themselves while getting her the best care.

"Of course, that makes sense," I said. Last week I'd researched facilities for Robert, confident the county would pay for his placement. If we didn't have those resources, we'd be in the same boat.

"What's your story?" the man asked. Michael explained that we had adopted our children through the department of social services. He didn't mention that we got a stipend to cover their therapy and the county would pay for Robert's care if we placed him at a residential treatment center. Compared to this poor family, we were fortunate.

The nurse returned and motioned us to follow her to a private interview room. "We've admitted Robert. He understands he will be here for three days and you'll come back during visiting hours. He asked that you bring his pillow and stuffed dog."

"What's going to happen to him?" Michael asked.

"We'll conduct some assessments and review the samples we took today to rule out drug use or any medical causes for erratic behavior. We'll prepare a report for you with recommendations for his ongoing treatment. I take it this is not the first episode of this kind?"

There was no way to summarize what we had been through with him over the past five years.

"Robert is our adopted foster child. He's had a lot of problems from day one. I understand you will be contacting his therapist to get his history and assessments," I said.

The nurse nodded in the weary way of someone who had heard the same story too many times. I felt we often got a free pass when we described our children's problems. No one blamed us, the saintly foster parents. But what about the other couple, whose birth child was mentally ill? Whom do they blame?

Michael and I drove home in silence, numbed and saddened by the circumstances and the limited options ahead. We were home alone for the first time in years. We both drank more these days and went through a couple of large jugs of wine every week. I hoped for sleep as I poured us full glasses of cheap Chablis. We wandered off to different parts of the house, Michael to the family room sofa where he often slept and me to our bedroom, each of us reading and drinking in the eerie quiet.

27

AT THE EDGE

The first thing I noticed was the patch on the wall, about the size of a fist, hovering over the bed as a testament to the previous occupant's frustration. Duct tape covered a tear in the carpet near the closet door, which hung askew off its track. There could have been an imaginary line drawn down the middle of the room, each half containing a twin bed, dresser, and lamp on a nightstand. Empty hangers hung from the dowel rod on Robert's side of the closet, but his roommate's clothes and toys encroached. Drawings and photos jammed a bulletin board along with memos and a list of rules.

The three of us stood in the doorway, holding boxes and duffel bags. The room looked more dismal than the model we had been shown during the tour. I worried we'd made a mistake bringing him here. Robert tossed the small bag he carried on the floor next to the bed and looked to see how much closet space he had. The only expression he wore was mild curiosity as he scanned the stuff piled on the floor, clues to the personality of his roommate. There was no reaction when we told him he would live at Edgewood Children's Center in San Francisco for a while, only resignation, as if everything was going to plan.

"Robert, I'm going to put your clothes in your dresser the same way we have at home, okay?" Michael said.

"I'll do it myself later."

Michael looked at me and shrugged.

"Let's get some of this unpacked," I said. "You have a group session in fifteen minutes and they want you there to introduce yourself."

"I'll put these boxes in the closet and you can decide where you want things," Michael said.

I pulled out Robert's quilt from home—his favorite, covered with baseball symbols—and draped it over his bed.

"I'll get that later, Mom. I'm not sure I want that blanket after all."

I folded the cover and put it on the dresser while Robert scanned his roommate's side of the closet to see what he wore and what toys he had. I wanted Robert to start off on the right foot, though I didn't worry about him fitting in. I'd always marveled at both of my children's ability to adapt. "Okay. We're just trying to help. Let's go over to the main building so we can be on time. Maybe you'll meet your new roommate there."

Touring Edgewood a month earlier, we had learned that the children stayed in shared bedrooms in residential cottages. Meals were brought to each home from a kitchen in the main building, a large white adobe structure that reminded me of the historic Presidio nearby. The spacious grounds had several playgrounds and athletic fields and a view of the ocean. We were lucky they had a bed available. The only other facility for Robert's age was overcrowded and in a bad neighborhood in Oakland.

By the time we arrived at the main building, the kids were assembled in a circle in the living room. Boys of all sizes and races piled on sofas or sat on the floor, chatting, shoving, and shouting. Two young men in their early twenties stood at the opening in the circle near two folding chairs in front of an unlit fireplace. One counselor, a white kid with dreads and wearing shorts and a Bob Marley T-shirt, made notations on a clipboard as the kids entered the room. Robert joined a couple of boys on the floor but kept his distance. An older boy noticed Michael and me standing and brought us folding chairs.

"Let's get started. Check-ins, please." The other counselor, an African American wearing Dockers and a polo shirt, leaned over and reminded him there was a new kid to introduce. "Oh, yeah, thanks, Joe. Robert, tell us about yourself."

Robert stiffened as everyone turned to him. I knew he didn't like the attention, and I felt anxious.

"My name's Robert."

"Tell us where you're from."

"Livermore."

"And what are your hobbies? What do you like to do?"

"I like sports. I'm a wrestler. I play right field in baseball." The boy next to him crooked his arm around Robert's neck in a fake hold.

"Hey, knock it off, Matt. Robert, why don't you introduce your parents?"

"They're not my real parents. Michael and Catherine are my foster parents."

Michael and I smiled and waved from our seats as heads turned toward us. I was used to our children pointing out we weren't their real parents. Sometimes it hurt my feelings, especially since the adoption was final and we'd been living as a family for six years. They liked to capitalize on the attention they got if they said they were foster kids.

"Thanks. Okay, Robert, you'll get the hang of this, but the first thing we do with our group session is check in. Marco, show him how it's done. Everyone say your name for Robert. Hey, settle down, guys." Side conversations had started during Robert's introduction.

"I'm Marco and I'm not feeling that great today," he said. "I lost my TV privileges because of something that was not my fault. I think I'm gonna file a grievance."

"Marco, we spent time during our last group talking about this. We know you're upset and you're welcome to file a grievance. Joe here can help you with that. Paul, you're next."

"I'm feeling fantastic 'cause I just got twenty points for *most improved* and I'm gonna spend it all on candy." Paul hopped on the sofa, whooping and pumping his arm in celebration. The other boys joined in.

"Way to go, Paul." The check-ins continued around the room. Some reported progress at school, others had complaints. The boy named Matt accused another of stealing and the counselors asked them to stay after to resolve the conflict. A latecomer tried to sneak into the meeting but was spotted and docked with a notation to the clipboard. The counselors made announcements and asked for volunteers to decorate the room for the party they held for everyone with a birthday during the month. The last item on the agenda was another go-around with each boy stating his goal for the coming week.

"Pass my math test."

"Get twenty points."

"Get my TV privileges back."

"Be on time to meetings," the latecomer said.

When it was Robert's turn to share his goal, he wasn't prepared. He looked at the counselors and shrugged. "We'll let you off the hook your first time, Robert. Next."

"Beat the crap outa Richard," the boy with the earlier grievance said.

"Hey, Matt, that's not cool. I said we'd resolve that." Joe motioned for the two boys to follow him while the other counselor adjourned the meeting and sent everyone else to their cottages for dinner.

We joined Robert and introduced ourselves to the remaining counselor, whose name we learned was Keith. We knew that dozens of these counselors rotated three-day, two-night shifts at the cottages, and they needed to know we'd be tracking Robert's progress.

"Do you understand the schedule?" Keith said. Robert nodded. On the drive to San Francisco we'd gone over the schedule and rules.

"You have to be on time for everything or you'll get docked," he said. "You're one of the few who's allowed to go to a regular school, so to keep that privilege you have to be back in time for chores, group, and meals. If you stay on track, you can earn points and use them to buy stuff at the store. You got that?" Robert nodded. "Good. By the way, hang around for a minute and I'll introduce you to your roommate, Matt."

Robert's eyes widened in alarm, and he glanced at us to make sure we had heard. Great—the one roughneck in the group rooms with Robert. He knew we were worried about leaving him there, so this news only exacerbated our guilt.

None of us spoke as we returned to the cottage. Robert led the way as Michael and I followed him back to his room. We took a different tack and asked him where he wanted things. I didn't object when he asked me to take the comforter back home. He was in charge of this new stage of his life. Defining the contents of his closet was a start.

After we finished helping Robert settle in, we joined everyone for dinner in the dining room. The din of table setting guided us to where several young boys scurried about dropping plates and silverware on the oilcloth-covered tables. One counselor supervised, correcting sloppiness and nudging the slowpokes. He introduced himself as Kevin and showed Robert the assignment chart for table setting and cleanup.

"You get a free pass tonight, Robert," he said. "But your name will be here with the others starting tomorrow. Those on cleanup duty can socialize in the playroom until the dinner bell. You're welcome to hang out there till six p.m."

Robert nodded and ambled across the room to where Kevin pointed. From the dining room we could see and hear half a dozen boys playing video games, cards, and a rousing game of ping pong.

"Mom and Dad, you can have a seat on those sofas until dinner," Kevin said.

I took a seat while Michael paced around the room. We agreed to stay for dinner, but Michael seemed anxious to get back on the road. I was keenly aware of a handoff of sorts. These nice young men were running the show now, and we needed to let them do their job and Robert find his place. I struggled with where we stood in all of this and wasn't ready to relax and let others take charge. Would Robert chafe at the restrictions? What if he stole from the other kids? Would he get beaten up? I fretted about these possible outcomes while observing the happy chaos of the cottage.

A few minutes later a gong sounded from the dining room. The boys poured out of the playroom while the ones on kitchen duty brought out the hot dishes. We followed them in and found a place to sit with Robert. Plates and bowls, heaping with mashed potatoes, fried chicken, and buttered peas, passed around while the boys at the table pelted Robert with questions.

"What grade are you in?"

"Hey, we can ride the bus together to school."

"Do you want to play a game of Super Mario Brothers after dinner?"

"What weight class are you in wrestling?"

"Where's Livermore?"

Robert's answers were barely audible, but a hint of a smile indicated he was pleased with the attention. He needed to make friends with these kids, and just as in the world outside these walls, if he messed with them, there'd be consequences.

After dinner, we said our good-byes. It would be two weeks before we could see him again. The plan was to immerse him in the routine, and then visits with the family could begin. We'd scheduled family therapy sessions with the psychologist and were told we could take him out to dinner or home for weekends if things went well.

On the way home, I started to imagine living again without worrying about what Robert was up to. What would life be like not having to check if he had stolen from us or concocted something dangerous? My normal state was constant alert. I had forgotten how to relax.

"Do you think he'll be all right?" I asked. I looked over at Michael, who was focused on merging onto the Bay Bridge. His lips tightened and he shook his head.

"Do we have a choice?" he said.

28

No Pizza

Tell Catherine and Michael how you feel. I'm sure they'll listen and not get mad." Ira, Robert's therapist at Edgewood Children's Center, had prepared us for this. He and Robert sat in office chairs, facing us seated on the couch.

Robert straightened himself as if steeling for an ordeal. "I never thought you wanted me. You just wanted Jenny and took me because you had to."

Did he really believe this? I wanted to shout, *"That's not true!"* but I didn't want to discourage Robert from speaking up. "Why do you feel that?" I asked. I was glad Jenny wasn't in this session.

"You were mad at me all the time. I was always being punished. It felt like you wanted to get rid of me. That you were sorry I was around."

"We were upset because you did scary stuff, Robert. And you stole from us all the time. What were we supposed to do?" Michael said.

Robert hung his head and dug at the carpet with his toe. I believed his behaviors were more like tests of our love than signs of his mental illness. I hated the idea that he believed we didn't want him, yet here he was—somewhere other than our home. Of course he felt we didn't want him.

"How are you feeling, Robert?" Ira asked.

"Sometimes I feel like an empty basket."

No one said a word. I knew what he meant. Sometimes, no matter what I did for these children, nothing was enough. For the past five years, they'd been the center of our world. We did everything we could think of to have a normal family life for them—dinners together, homework, chores, camping, and holidays. Nothing made up for those lost early years. Now we were acting as Robert's scapegoat so he could heal from his birth family's neglect. It was too much to bear.

"Robert, I can't think of anything else to do for you," I said. I reached for the Kleenex box on the coffee table between us. "I love you so much, but I can't figure out how else to help you."

The tears came. There was a knot in my chest. A tear rolled down Robert's cheek when he saw my face. He walked over and put an arm around my shoulder. "It's okay, Mom. I know you tried."

Robert and I held each other for a few moments while Ira waited. Michael crossed his arms and glared at Ira while I struggled to stop sobbing. This was supposed to be Robert's session and I needed to get control of myself.

"Robert, all we want is for you to come home so we can be a family again," I said. We did miss Robert, but I didn't miss having to be in hypervigilant mode, wondering if he was doing something dangerous or stealing. The past month, I had started to relax at home and discovered I had more energy for Jenny.

"That's enough for today," Ira said. "Why don't you two wait outside for a minute while I talk to Robert." Michael and I left the room and joined Jenny, who was next door supposedly doing her homework. She was working on a coloring book instead.

"Do you want to get some pizza?" I asked.

"Sure." She hopped out of her chair, ready to go, but then noticed my puffy face and the Kleenex in my hand. "Are you okay, Mom?"

I kissed the top of her head as she hugged me. In spite of the rough start these children had, I marveled at their capacity for empathy. I glanced over at my husband, who stood at the window frowning as he surveyed the playground. "I'll be fine, Honey. It's hard with Robert. Sometimes I feel sad because I can't help him."

"Is he coming with us to Paradise Pizza? It's my turn to pick the pizza, you know."

"He's coming," I said. On cue, the door to Ira's office opened.

"Robert has something else he needs to share with you," Ira said. "Robert?"

"I'm on restriction and can't leave," Robert said.

"What happened?" I asked.

"What?" Michael turned from the window.

"Matt said I stole his video game," Robert said.

"And what else?" Ira prompted.

"A couple of other kids said I stole stuff from them too, which isn't true. They're just looking for someone to blame 'cause they lost their stuff."

"Robert had to sit in group and hear from the others how they felt about him stealing their things. Some of them were pretty angry, and he's not yet ready to accept responsibility for his actions."

All I could say was "Oh, Robert." Michael shook his head and returned to staring out the window. "I guess this means he's not going to dinner with us." he said.

"I'm afraid not. He's got extra chores helping out with the yardwork." *Just like home,* I thought. Jenny tried to hug Robert good-bye, but he winced and kept his arms at his side.

"Hopefully he can come home for Easter weekend," I said.

Ira placed his hand on Robert's shoulder. "Sound like a plan, Robert?"

Robert looked up at him and nodded. Did he want to come home?

❖

Robert stayed at Edgewood Children's Center for almost nine months. The rigid routine, psychotherapy, and twenty-four-hour supervision seemed to do him good. He appeared to be happier and more confident and was looking forward to coming home. When Robert was discharged, we made an effort to start him out with a clean slate. We didn't want to have to supervise him like we had before, so we agreed to allow Robert to visit with friends after school and go to the store on his own.

But I couldn't help but worry. These days I was super alert, watching for any danger signs from Robert and avoiding Michael's bad temper. I escaped this stress through work, busying myself with the nonprofit I had started in addition to my contract work. At night, I found I needed more wine to help me sleep. The master bedroom was all mine now. Michael continued to blame me for the bad turn his life had taken, and he punished me by sulking at dinner and sleeping on the couch.

29

No Visible Scars

I t looks like nothing's broken, but I think you'll be sore for a while." The doctor studied me as I balanced myself on the edge of the hospital bed. I grew embarrassed under his gaze. Landing in the emergency room with injuries caused by my husband was something from a soap opera, not my life.

"Well, that's good news," I said. I focused on finding my shoes and purse. "I guess I can go?" Robert and Jenny had been in the waiting room adjacent to the emergency room of the Walnut Creek Kaiser Hospital for a couple of hours and it was a school night.

"I can have the front desk get an officer in here if you want to file a police report."

I rummaged through my purse, making sure my Kaiser card was back in my wallet.

"Thanks, but I'm not going to do that tonight. I need to get the kids settled."

"You're not going home, are you?" I appreciated his concern, but I wasn't one of those women, a helpless victim who needed someone to guide them to do the right thing.

"No, I'm not sure what's going on there. I'll get a hotel room."

"All right, then. Here's something for the pain." He tore a sheet from his prescription pad. "Watch for other symptoms—dizziness, maybe nausea. Make an appointment with your doctor for follow-up in a week."

Jenny and Robert were watching David Letterman on the small

television suspended from the ceiling. When Jenny saw me she jumped up and hugged me tightly around my bruised ribs. I bent down and kissed her head, hoping she hadn't seen me wince, but Robert had, and he pulled Jenny away. "Don't hurt Mom," he said.

"Are you okay?" Jenny asked.

"I'm okay, Honey."

"Is Daddy in trouble? Is he going to jail?"

Robert turned back to the television. "He shouldn't have done that," he said.

"You're right. Dad needs some help to figure this out. He won't do this again."

"I don't want to go home. I'm scared," Jenny said.

"Daddy's not mad at you and he would never hurt you. You don't have to worry."

Robert looked at me, then back at the television. He'd been through this with his birth parents and was not reassured.

"We'll do something different tonight. We'll stay in a hotel. It'll be an adventure." I'd used the term *adventure* for a ferry ride to Sausalito. These kids were too smart for that.

"We don't have our pajamas," Jenny said.

"That's part of the adventure," Robert said.

While waiting for the X-ray results, I'd pondered my options, including a domestic violence shelter in Livermore, but that was for poor women who had no resources. I had a credit card and my own income, and I knew what to do. I'd warned Michael if he hurt me again, he would leave me no choice but to call the police. There was a chance he would lose his job over this, but it had to stop.

The next morning I drove by the house and saw that Michael's car was gone. The kids got cleaned up and left for school while I called the police department to find out the procedure. Two hours later a female officer met me at the house to file the report.

"So, have these kinds of incidents happened before?" she asked. The stocky young woman sat on the edge of the sofa, burdened by all the equipment hanging from her belt.

"I'm afraid so, a few times. He gave me a black eye once. Another time, he punched my arm. It's been a while since the last incident, and he was seeing a psychologist for his anger management. I didn't really expect this."

"Has he ever hurt the children?"

"Never. Just me." *Lucky me*, I thought. Michael had so many issues to work out, and I got to be his whipping post.

"What triggered the incident?"

"I'm not really sure. He gets in these dark moods and it's easy to say something that sets him off. I think we were arguing about money."

"Are you safe staying here? Will he try to hurt you? There is a shelter in Livermore, you know."

Here it comes: you poor, helpless victim. I was determined to get on top of this myself. I just wanted to file the report and scare him into leaving me alone.

"Knowing him, I think he's cooled off. I think he's scared he'll be arrested."

"I can take this report and he will be arrested if you want to press charges. Is that what you want to do?"

I stared at the paperwork, reading the statement over the line where she asked me to sign. *If he's arrested, he'll lose his job, our main source of income.*

"What do you want to do next?" she asked.

I had given this a lot of thought, researched apartments nearby, and drawn up a budget for being on my own. I had income and contracts for work for various businesses and nonprofits, but it wasn't enough to support the three of us. The small stipend we got from the county barely covered the kids' therapy. I knew what furniture and household goods I'd take and had opened my own checking account months ago, but the charge cards were maxed and we owed a second on the house. The timing was not good. There had to be a way I could leave without sinking into a financial quagmire.

"I don't want him arrested. He'll lose his job and we need him employed."

"All right, well, here's our list of marriage and family counselors. When Mr. Sievert returns he needs to know, if there's a second complaint, he will be arrested, regardless of whether you file a report."

"I don't believe this will happen again. He knows I'm serious."

She paused at the door and gave me a weary look. "Yeah, well, there's always a first time."

Michael returned home two days later. He'd been camping at Del Valle, hiding in fear of being arrested. He looked drawn and stressed, like a man who'd been spending his nights worrying about his future. I felt the scales tip in my favor. I could use this fear to manage him, control the situation till the time was right to leave. He tried to avoid me before he went to work, but agreed to meet at home later while the children were in school. I wasn't expecting an apology, but I wanted to hear if he had a plan to make sure this wouldn't happen again.

We sat in the family room, he on the love seat and me across the room on the sofa. The police report lay beside him. I looked out the patio door at the scruffy marigolds in the planter box, the patchy lawn, and the white oleanders in front of the brick wall separating our yard from the street behind us. He had no plan, only more complaints, so I tuned him out. I continued to stare out at the backyard. I noticed the city maintenance crew had drastically pruned back the sycamores that lined the street. I hated that look, but they thought it kept the roots from cracking the sidewalk.

Something he said caught my attention. "No one else would want you, you know. You're such an ugly woman."

For some reason, this made me smile. I focused on the sycamores and their hopeful growth in the spring in spite of the bad pruning. At that instant, I knew everything would be all right. I didn't need to work so hard to keep this family together. I would be fine and the kids would be fine. Jenny and Robert needed to know that everyone has the right to be treated well. It was important to show them I deserved to be loved.

"If you hurt me again, you're going to jail."

Michael said nothing else. He left the room and started fixing dinner, and I walked across the street to collect the kids from their after-school program.

30

MOVING MOUNTAINS

The classroom had been rearranged to make room for a semicircle of plastic chairs. The school principal, his secretary, the special education program supervisor, Robert's teacher, and the school psychologist were seated there. Michael and I were placed in the center, separate from the others as if we were interviewing for a job or facing a firing squad. This demonstration of solidarity was needed to deal with us, the pushy parents who requested and were being denied special education services for our son.

The principal began the meeting by smiling all around. His teal sport jacket and matching tie made his teeth gleam. "Mr. and Mrs. Sievert, I want you to know that we've given careful consideration to your request." He paused and gestured to his colleagues. "We certainly sympathize with your situation, but we have no indicators that Robert qualifies for the supervised special education program. He performs well academically and, with the exception of a couple of minor incidents, we've experienced no behavior problems with him."

"So you need this meeting to tell us that? Why are we here then?" I asked. I was battle weary and had no patience for this politically correct show of authority. Michael shot me a look that told me I sounded like a crazy woman. Not a good start, but I pressed on.

"Look, I know you have a lot of kids here, and special education with the restricted classroom is an extraordinary intervention, but we've provided mounds of evidence that show this is the best placement for him."

I pointed to the file box that we had carted from home. It held copies of Robert's psychological assessments and the recommendations from the psychiatric hospital, social services, his therapists, and Edgewood. "If he attends the regular classroom he won't have the supervision he needs and he'll get into trouble. Then we'll all have to deal with the juvenile justice system."

The school psychologist, a bookish young woman wearing a pink silk blouse with a ridiculous large bow, whispered to the principal. The others looked down at their notes, avoiding eye contact.

I continued. "You saw what happened at Edgewood. At first, he was allowed to go to the local school, but then he went truant and stole from local stores. Edgewood had to keep him at their on-campus school and he did really well there. We want him to continue his therapy and give him the best chance at finishing middle school."

The psychologist intervened, taking her boss out of my line of fire. "Mrs. Sievert, we have to follow district regulations. Unless Robert has committed a crime and the juvenile courts require it or his Individual Education Plan indicates the need for special education, he doesn't qualify for these services."

"Even if his psychologist and his social worker agree this is the best strategy?" I said. I wasn't going to make this easy for them. What we had was a misalignment of the state department of mental health, county social services, and the school district. Robert hadn't demonstrated to the school he was a danger, so they weren't going to take this precautionary measure.

Michael piped in. "I would like to suggest that the only reason Robert hasn't been a problem at school is because we monitor him constantly. We check his backpack and escort him to and from school. You recall he's not allowed in the after-school program because of the incident last year."

The principal and Robert's teacher looked puzzled. They hadn't read the application in detail so I saw a chance to make a point. "It's in the report." I said. "We had to '5150' him last year for threatening to set a child's hair on fire."

The psychologist jumped in, getting her boss off the hook. "Technically that incident happened while he was under the supervision of the parks and recreation program. The district wasn't involved."

"So what you're saying is he can do dangerous things outside the school and you don't care as long as the district's not involved?" Everyone looked at their notes again except for the psychologist, who pursed her lips in disapproval of my sarcastic tone.

I continued. "Last week, Robert was acting suspicious as he was heading off for school, so I checked his backpack. I found a Coleman stove propane canister and some matches. It looked like some kind of bomb. Would you rather we weren't so vigilant so he qualifies for your services?" I did sound like a crazy woman. I was a little embarrassed and quite desperate.

"I'm sorry. There isn't anything we can do at this point," the principal said. He looked sympathetic, but I wasn't the first parent he'd said *no* to.

"Perhaps the Sieverts would like us to provide them with a list of resources to improve their parenting skills," the psychologist said. We were used to this, insinuations that our children's problems were due to bad parenting. I wanted to tighten her bow. I'd had enough.

"That won't be necessary," I said. I rose to leave and Michael followed, taking the luggage cart with the box of files. He turned to face the group, not wanting to leave on a bad note. "Thank you for your time," he said.

Over the next few months, Robert skipped school and raided local stores, stealing a number of things including more than thirty BIC lighters. How he avoided getting caught was a mystery. I believe that if he'd been in the restricted special education program, we could have kept him home with us, but his dangerous behaviors left us fearing for our lives. Less than a year after he was discharged, we readmitted Robert to Edgewood. We gave up any hope of keeping him at home. The best we could do was to make sure he had the help he needed to stay safe and out of jail.

31

Just When I Thought the Coast Was Clear

Are you sure you want to spend all your birthday money here?" I asked.
Jenny fingered the price tag on the designer shorts outfit displayed
on the boutique rack. "If we go to Target, you can buy lots of clothes for
the same amount of money." We were celebrating her twelfth birthday
with lunch and shopping at the mall. I realized I was being a wet blanket
and changed my approach. "You decide, Honey. You can use your birthday money any way you want."

"Target," she said.

"Are you sure?" Maybe she was trying to please me? At least she still
cared what I thought.

"Yeah, but let's get an Orange Julius before we go, okay?"

"Good idea."

We walked through the mall, which was crowded with Saturday
shoppers and kids Jenny's age. Little herds of middle-schoolers jostled
on the escalators, poking each other and giggling at things they thought
were funny. Compared to most of them, my daughter was lovely, poised
and tall for her age. Her long, strawberry blond hair framed her freckled
face and blue-green eyes. Some kids she knew waved at her from an opposite balcony.

"Can I go over and say *Hi*, Mom?"

"Sure. I'll wait over there." I pointed to the oasis of sofas usually
occupied by men waiting for their wives or kids to finish shopping. As
she hurried to her friends, I watched heads turn: teenage boys, dads with

strollers, and men older than me. I wanted to shout, *"She's only twelve years old, for god's sake!"*

Jenny and I lived alone now. Robert was in a group home in San Francisco, a place we chose together so he could attend a high school he liked. He had outgrown Edgewood and still needed the supervision we were unable to give him at home.

Michael had moved out about the same time, shortly after his father passed away. A small inheritance paid off our bills with enough cash left for a down payment for his condo in Oakland. We were both more relaxed with our finances improved and made an effort to separate amicably. We shopped together to set up his household, and in a gesture of goodwill he repainted the interior of our home before he left. We agreed not to divorce right away so that I could stay on his insurance. I now had a full-time job that required a commute to San Francisco and occasional travel, so we needed to cooperate to manage our parenting of Jenny and our family visits with Robert. Once Michael was gone, I filled the cupboards with my favorite foods and bought myself some new clothes. I felt I could breathe again and looked forward to having fun with Jenny.

The day after our shopping trip, Jenny planned to meet a few friends to celebrate her birthday. I dropped her off at the skating rink in Dublin and gave her twenty dollars for her entry fee and snacks. She was dressed in her usual jeans, T-shirt, and sneakers, and her hair was wound in a sloppy ponytail with a pink scrunchy. I had let her wear mascara and lipstick for the special occasion. She kissed me good-bye, flung her backpack over her shoulder, and headed off to join her friends. We agreed to meet in the parking lot in three hours.

I used the time to grocery shop and pick up sprinkler parts at the hardware store. Our twenty-year-old ranch house was getting the best of me, so I spent most weekends doing handyman chores. I didn't want to drive all the way back to Livermore, so I returned to the rink early, planning to hang out on the sidelines till Jenny was finished skating with her friends.

It took a moment to adjust my eyes from the bright sunlight to the dark interior. The clanging of video games competed with the pulsing disco music, and the smell of popcorn reminded me I was hungry. I shaded my eyes from the flashing strobes to view the skating area filled with teenagers, children, and a few adults circling the rink. A handsome couple skated like professionals, dancing gracefully around parents holding their toddlers upright.

From a distance, one skater looked out of place in the wholesome setting. She wore white cut-off jeans and a shirt torn off at the midriff with the neck pulled down, baring her shoulders and exposing her bra straps. Close behind her were a couple of college-age boys who, by their gestures, seemed fascinated by the thong underwear peeking over the tight shorts. I wondered what this floozy was doing here and whom she was with. As she rounded the circle and skated toward me, I saw her heavily made-up face, clownlike with red lipstick and rouged cheeks. Her eyes, encircled with heavy eye liner, widened as she spotted me. I crooked my finger in a *Come here* signal, and she rolled off the main floor to where I stood. I was determined not to make a scene. I was embarrassed by Jenny's appearance and didn't want to call any more attention to her.

"Get your things. We're going home," I said. She skated over to her friends to retrieve her backpack, pointing at me as I stood with my arms crossed. They nodded solemnly. An angry mother needed no explanation.

Once in the car, I let her have it. "What were you thinking? Where did you get that slutty outfit? You looked like a hooker." I was angry and disappointed. I felt I no longer knew my daughter. It was as if she had a secret life. Jenny knew I had caught her in a deception, so she had little to say, and I didn't give her a chance to answer. On the drive home, she slumped in her seat and scowled, though I caught her smirking when she thought I wasn't looking.

When we arrived home, I told her to wash the makeup off her face. Meanwhile I dumped the contents of her dresser bureau on her bed. When she returned to her room, I held up the pretty peasant top we'd bought the day before. It had been crudely scissored to just below the bra line.

"What did you do to your new blouse?"

"It's my outfit. I bought it with my birthday money. You said I could do what I want with it, remember?" Jenny plopped down on her bed next to the pile and propped herself up on her elbows. She looked amused by my distress.

"And where did you get these?" Thong underwear and a push-up bra rolled from a balled up sweater.

"I borrowed those. I have to give them back?"

"You borrowed underwear? Never mind. Whose mother lets them buy these?"

Jenny lay back on the bed and stared at the ceiling. "I'll give them back."

"If your friends want these back, they have to ask me for them. I don't trust you to return them."

"Mom!" It was Jenny's turn to look distressed.

"What are you thinking when you dress like this? Don't you know men as old as your Dad are leering at you? Is that what you want?"

"No."

"What are you going to do if a big old guy starts bothering you when you're dressed like this?"

"I don't know."

Alarm bells were clanging in my head. I imagined every mother of a teenage girl goes through a tug-of-war about looking more grown up. I remembered haggling with my mother about the height of my first high-heeled dress shoe. But this was different, or at least I thought it was. Jenny had the intellectual and emotional maturity of a ten-year-old and was not equipped to handle any problems caused by the way she dressed. And the way she dressed went far beyond pushing the boundaries about a proper dress shoe. It was clear she wanted to get male attention by dressing slutty and was willing to break my trust to get it.

After sorting through the piles of clothes and removing the items I thought were indecent, I asked her to put everything back in her dresser and stay in her room for the rest of the evening. I told her she had to think about what she had done, but the truth was I didn't want to see or talk to her. I needed to think. We'd had the talk about sex and babies over a year ago, but I could see I was going to have to do more, perhaps go over how to use condoms and avoid sexually transmitted diseases. I would also have to teach her how to say *no* and call for help if she got in over her head. Jenny's charm and willingness to please were sweet traits when she was a toddler, but her lack of boundaries was a magnet for sleazebags.

I poured myself a glass of wine and made a cheese and cracker plate, my favorite supper when I ate alone. I'd splurged on a nice bottle since I didn't have to share it. As I sipped, I allowed myself to sink into a warm bath of self-pity. *Damn it all. I just wanted a break for once.*

32

LOST IN THE HAIGHT

I walked among the dirty sleeping bags and blankets, cautiously peering at the prone bodies. Many of them resembled my son: thin white teenage kids, dirty and sleepy-looking or stoned. A young girl with blond dreadlocks glared. Someone like me, a middle-aged mom, was out of place and unwelcome. I steered clear of the huddles that were guarded by dogs or surrounded by shopping carts. Some of the older men wore layers of coats, streaked with filth and smelling of sweat and urine. My son had been missing from his group home for only a few days, so I didn't think he had settled into this life in the Haight-Ashbury as some here seemed to be.

I headed back down the hill toward the head shops and hippie clothing stores, determined to distribute the rest of my homemade flyers to whomever would post them. Earlier, when I'd showed his photo to the store clerks along the street, few bothered to look at it, pointing to their bulletin boards already filled with flyers of missing children.

I knew this effort to find my son was a waste of time, but it was something I could do instead of waiting for the police to call. The director of the group home thought Robert might be hanging out in the Haight because he'd wandered there the last two times he'd run away. It was known to be a good place to panhandle and get quick cash from tourists. Four days after Robert went missing, the director called. "They've found him," she said.

"Where is he?"

"The Berkeley police have him at their station on Martin Luther King near the campus. They picked him up in People's Park."

I sat down on the couch by the phone, relieved and anxious. Her somber voice told me there was more I needed to know.

"Is he all right? Can I go get him or are you supposed to?"

"I think you and your husband better go see him," she said. "They're saying he may have been molested. They picked him up with a pedophile who's known to hang around with skateboarders and homeless kids. The police are questioning Robert to see if they have enough to build a case."

My ears buzzed and the room grew dark. I collapsed onto the love seat and made an effort to breathe.

"Are you there?"

"Give me a second." I fumbled for a pen and paper and asked her to repeat the name of the officer and the address of the police station.

When we got off the phone, I took a moment to gather my thoughts. I pushed away the idea that my son may have been abused by a predator. I called Michael before he left work, asking him to pick Jenny up from school and meet me at the police station.

"Does he have any idea what we've been through?" Michael said. "We've been worried sick, staying by the phone in case the police called. Is he all right?"

"That's just it. The police think he may have been molested. They're interviewing him now and holding the guy he was with."

"Dear God. What else can happen?"

We were having difficulty dealing with this, but we had to hurry to the police station. I gave Michael the address and agreed to meet him there once he got Jenny.

When we met in the lobby, Jenny was clinging to Michael, looking worried. "Is Robert in jail, Mom?" she asked.

"No, Honey. He's not in trouble. They want to talk to him for a while before we take him back to San Francisco. We'll see him when they're finished. We might have to wait a while. Did you bring your homework?"

Jenny took off her backpack and slumped down in the plastic chair beside me. Michael sat beside her and looked up at me. When our eyes connected I saw the same misery and despair I felt. His face sagged with weariness, and he slouched in a defeated heap. Nothing needed to be said. We'd been down this path so many times, we were numb.

"Mr. and Mrs. Sievert."

Michael and I turned to the officer who spoke to us from the counter. "Would you step over here, please?" he said.

"We finished interviewing Robert. I'm afraid he hasn't been able to help us very much. He may have been drugged, or stoned, so he can't remember what happened. We've detained the guy he was with because the San Francisco PD had an arrest warrant on him for something similar. Robert may have to testify later."

"Can we talk to him now?" Michael asked.

"That's just it. He says he doesn't want to talk to you. We understand the situation from the group home and I sympathize, but we can't force him to speak to you. We'll be taking him back to the group home in San Francisco in a few minutes."

"Okay. We expected this, I guess," Michael said.

"Wait—what?" I asked. I leaned forward on the counter, but Michael took my elbow and steered me away before I could object further.

"Aren't we going to see Robert now?" Jenny asked.

"No, we can't, Jenny, sorry," Michael said. "Get your stuff so Mom can take you home." Michael let go of my arm to help Jenny zip up her backpack. She looked at me and started to cry. I was near tears myself so Jenny knew something was terribly wrong. I was tired of being stoic when the situation was so hopeless. The years of trying to protect Robert and help him recover had weighed me down.

"Sorry, Jenny. We can't see him right now." I said. "The police thought it best they take him back to San Francisco. We'll go visit him this weekend, okay?"

I didn't have the heart to tell her the truth, that Robert wanted nothing to do with us. Even though there was little in his life under his control, he could control this. He had to know his refusal to see us would hurt and punish us. Robert had lots of reasons for exacting punishment. For now we were the bull's-eye. I understood this, but it was painful to be on the receiving end, to take the hit for the abuse and neglect that happened way before we came into his life.

We walked out of the station toward the parking lot as the police car pulled out of the garage. Robert, sitting in the back seat, turned to look out the window. At first his eyes lit up when he spotted us, but then he smiled and turned away. All three of us stared helplessly as he rode by. We stood in silence while we waited for the traffic to clear and held hands as we crossed the street together.

33

SOLOMON AGAIN

We got lost driving on the country road near Auburn. Jenny did her best to read the directions, but we turned the wrong way and had to back up the winding road to the fork we'd missed. We found the number on the mailbox and headed down the gravel driveway toward the small, tidy home at the end. Two vehicles were parked in front, one a decade-old Ford F-150 with the hood up. A garage and an outbuilding had the same light blue siding as the main house. The metal roof was covered with debris from the nearby sycamores and pines. It was November, and it was cooler in the Sierra foothills than in Livermore. Even though it was sunny, I was glad we'd brought our heavier jackets. The screen door opened and my son stepped onto the porch. It had been almost two years since I'd seen him. He waved like a good host and pointed to where we should park.

Jenny unsnapped her seat belt and rushed up the porch steps to embrace her brother. Robert looked pleased and embarrassed as he hugged her back and smiled at me over Jenny's shoulder. He wore a trucker's cap, wire-rim glasses, and a scruffy little mustache most seventeen-year-old boys would be proud of. When he hugged me he seemed taller but just as thin as before. He held the door for us as we entered the dark interior. Lisa Clyde's mother, seated in a brown upholstered recliner near the single lit lamp, extended her hand to greet me. Robert reminded her who I was, and she smiled in the vague way of someone not quite sure where she was. Jenny kissed her and called her Grandma—Jenny had met her before during a visit with her birth mother the previous Christmas. Today Lisa Clyde was nowhere around. If she had been, she'd have gotten a piece of my mind.

After the incident with the pedophile, Robert ran away from the group home again, this time for good. A year and a half later his birth mother tried to collect welfare benefits for him and the social security number she provided to Placer County DSS linked to a juvenile reported missing in San Francisco. Lisa Clyde had to explain her actions to the local police and social services.

When I had first learned Robert was alive and safe, I was relieved—and then very angry. I had spent months worrying about him, checking with the police and scanning kids' faces in crowds in the futile hope I'd find him on my own. During that time I'd taken Jenny to visit with her birth mother many times, not knowing Lisa Clyde was hiding him nearby. It was now clear she had used the earlier court-ordered family visits to encourage my children to run away. It was inexcusable for her to hide him when she knew I was heartsick with worry. To this day, I've found it hard to forgive her.

When I began the process of bringing Robert back to the Bay Area, I was stunned to learn that Alameda County DSS would not support his return. They considered him a runaway risk and a liability for the county and didn't want to devote the resources to housing him again. For months I haggled with the family court and the social service agencies of both counties. I knew Lisa Clyde was incapable of caring for Robert. Since the children's adoption she'd been homeless numerous times and was rarely employed. It was only recently that her mother had allowed Lisa to stay with her.

The grandmother's tiny three-bedroom housed four adults and two children, including a fourth child of the Clydes conceived during a prison conjugal visit. Because Robert was older, the courts took his wishes into consideration, and he wanted to stay in Auburn with his birth family. Lisa Clyde promised the courts that Robert would attend school and stay out of trouble. As his adoptive parents, Michael and I had to agree to the arrangement. I wasn't convinced it was the best choice for him, and I capitulated only after the court required extra supervision and reports on Robert's well-being. I felt defeated by this turn of events. After all we had done to adopt Robert and make sure he had the best of care, he had ended up back with his birth mother. I called him often to check on his progress, and I was glad he had agreed to this visit.

Jenny sat next to her brother on the sofa so she could keep hold of his arm.

"So how's school so far?" I asked. " I saw your report card and some grades are great and others, not so much."

"I got an A in art, Robert," Jenny said.

"That's good, Jenny. I didn't do so well in English. I'm not really good at writing. I didn't do a couple of assignments and it brought my grade down." Robert attended an alternative high school with an independent study program that allowed him to make up the credits he had missed while on the run. It pained me to see him enrolled in this unchallenging environment when he could qualify for the gifted program as he had in Livermore.

"You know writing is pretty important for any job that pays well," I said. I was getting in as much parenting as I could during this short visit. "Have you thought more about going to college like we last talked about?"

"Well ... I just want to get through this year and then I'll think about it." I could tell he was humoring me, though I'd told both children I would help them through college and had savings set aside for that.

"So tell us about your job. Do you like working at the nursery?"

"So what's your name again?" Robert's grandmother pointed at me and started to stand.

"It's okay, Grammy. I told you about her." Robert rose quickly and helped her back into her chair. "We're just visiting for a while." He turned his attention back to me. "I really like it. I work fifteen hours a week, sometimes twenty, and they said they'd hire me full time once I graduate." Robert's face brightened as he talked about his responsibilities at the wholesale nursery where he worked. "I'm in charge of watering all the plants, and they're going to let me make deliveries once I'm eighteen."

"Robert, I'm taking the bus to the high school now. You know I'm a freshman, right?"

"I know, Jenny. Catherine told me." It jarred me to hear him call me by my name instead of *Mom*.

"Who are you?" Robert's grandmother looked alarmed. Robert got up again and patted her arm. "Why don't we get you to lie down for a nap?" he said. He helped her latch on to her walker and then escorted her to a back bedroom.

"Mom, can Robert come visit us?" Jenny asked while they were gone.

"If he wants to. We can ask if he'd like to ride the bus to Livermore for a visit during spring break."

"I miss him. I wish he wasn't so far away."

"Me too."

Robert returned to the sofa next to Jenny. He didn't seem to mind that she wanted to sit so close, and he smiled at her as she clung to his arm.

"I see you take good care of your grandma."

"She's better today. Sometimes she can't get out of bed."

"Does Lisa help?" I'd never identified her as his mom, and wasn't about to start.

"Grandpa Mike takes care of her mostly. He took Mom and little Karl into town so we could have this visit." *He calls her Mom now.*

"So, you still like to cook?" I asked.

"I do all the cooking here," he said. "I'm organizing the Thanksgiving dinner and I'm making everything from the stuffing to the pie." He smiled broadly as he described his menu plans. He was proud of his ability to cook, something he had learned at home from us. I could tell he wanted to impress me. He looked at peace, in charge of caring for his grandmother and, I had to assume, his mother and little brother. Perhaps these responsibilities were good for him, helping him mature.

"I want to come." Jenny looked hurt she wasn't invited to the feast.

"Honey, we're going to have Thanksgiving dinner at Daddy's house." She made a pouty face.

"Come on, let's take some pictures," I said. I needed a distraction from the idea we'd have to leave soon. If we made this first visit painful for Robert, he wouldn't want to see us again. I was satisfied just to see that he was doing okay and that Jenny had a chance to reconnect with him. I pulled the camera out of my purse and stood back to get them both in the frame. Robert wrapped his arms around Jenny and grinned at me while she smiled up at him. We went outside for more photos until a cold breeze reminded us it was time to go. Robert promised to call, and Jenny said she wanted to write him a letter. We hugged good-bye. Jenny wouldn't let go until I told her it was my turn. I patted his back and kissed his cheek and told him I wanted him to work hard in school.

"Love you," I said as I climbed in the car.

"Love you too," he said.

Jenny shouted more good-byes out the window as I focused on backing the car out of the driveway. Tears clouded my eyes as I gave him one more wave before we turned down the road.

34

WHAT GOES AROUND

She wasn't at school today, Tiffany. They called and said she was truant. Where is she?"

"I don't know. Why ask me? I thought she went to school."

"Really? You didn't go together?"

"No. She wanted to go on her own, I guess. I'm not her babysitter." Tiffany snorted at her own joke.

"Let me speak to your mother."

"She's at work."

"Well, when does she come home? I need to talk to her about this."

"My mom's not around. I gotta go." The line disconnected.

I grunted with frustration and hung up the phone. I'd allowed Jenny an overnight with her girlfriend as a reward for helping me shampoo the carpets. She and Tiffany were supposed to get themselves to school in the morning, a short walk from her house, but the message on my answering machine from the high school let me know that hadn't happened. I was foolish to trust my daughter again after numerous letdowns. Now it was seven o'clock, starting to get dark, and I didn't know where Jenny was or where she'd been all day.

It was difficult to keep my problems with Robert from affecting how I parented Jenny. I was determined not to lose another child and worried that I was overly vigilant with her. But Jenny had given me a number of reasons not to trust her. She'd disappeared often in the past year, once when she was supposed to be at her Girl Scout meeting and another time during an off-campus band recital. Though all she did was go off with her girlfriends, it was clear she enjoyed the attention she got when she went missing. This year, she had been truant from school so often she was in danger of having to repeat her freshman year. Her teacher had recently told me some of her classmates saw her hanging out with a rough group of older boys. I was going to have to do a little of detective work to find out where my daughter was.

Tiffany looked surprised to see me at her front door. The TV blared in the background, and I wasn't sure she was alone.

"Let's start over. Where's Jenny?" I asked.

"I told you, I don't know."

"I don't believe you."

She sniffed and looked away. "This isn't my problem," she said. She tried to close the door, but I straight-armed it before she could.

"Tell me where she is." I kept my voice low, but added a menacing tone I hoped she picked up. "You know, if something happens to her, you could be held responsible. Like an accessory to a crime." I knew this was over the top, but I was desperate.

Her eyes widened in fear. "Okay. She went with this guy. He's a senior she's been hanging out with. He showed up last night, him and his friends."

"Friends?"

"There were a lot of people in the car—boys. I don't know how many."

"And how do I find this guy, Tiffany? What's his name?"

She shrugged.

"Tiffany, I haven't filed a police report yet. Shall I have them come by and get this information from you?"

"His name is Darian, Darian Schultz. I got his number on a slip of paper Jenny left." She let go of the door and stomped off to her bedroom, and I used it as an excuse to enter the house. I wasn't leaving till I had what I needed. When she returned I thanked her. "You've been a big help," I said.

She knew I was being sarcastic and scowled. "Jenny's gonna be pissed," she said.

I drove home to check my messages and plan my next move. I was not naïve. Driving off with a carload of boys meant drugs, alcohol, and sex. I hadn't filed a police report, hoping I could keep Jenny out of trouble, but I needed help. I'd left a message with Michael earlier to see if he had heard from her, but there was nothing from him or Jenny. I thought about how I had bullied Tiffany into giving me the information I needed, and I felt ashamed, but that didn't deter me from trying the strategy again.

I checked the phone book reference section and saw that the phone number Tiffany had given me was in Concord, another San Francisco suburb about thirty miles away. I dialed and got an outgoing recorded message accompanied by punk metal music so loud I couldn't hear what was said. I hung up without leaving a message. I called five minutes later, let the message play, and hung up again. I did this repeatedly until I got what I wanted—a pick-up.

"Fuck. Who is this?"

"Darian?" I tried the low, calm, menacing tone I used with Tiffany.

"Who wants to know?"

"I'm Jenny's mother. I am on the way over to the police department to file a missing persons report."

"What's that got to do with me?"

"That depends. You know she's barely thirteen, right? Are you aware of the consequences for statutory rape in California?"

A hand covered the receiver and a muffled conversation ensued.

"Darian?"

"Yeah."

"There's a BART station nearby, right?"

"Yeah."

"Put her on it in the next thirty minutes."

"Yeah, okay."

I knew the BART ride from Concord would take at least forty minutes, so I had some time to think. Jenny was out of control, but lots of teenagers got out of control. Was this normal, or was she going down the same path as her brother? Her therapist had told me Jenny was very immature for her age and that there was a chance she had inherited her birth parents' tendencies toward mental illness and addictions. All of this plus her learning disabilities left her vulnerable to exploitation. She needed lots of help and supervision—which no teenager wants. I was confused and worried and hadn't the slightest idea how to help her. When I was her age, I was babysitting other people's children, and Kayla was never a worry like this. All I could think to do was impose more restrictions until she could be trusted again or she grew out of this, whatever *this* was. But I couldn't enforce any rules I set because both Michael and I worked full time.

As I drove to the Pleasanton BART station, I mentally reorganized my schedule for the next day. I'd have to take her to Kaiser to see if she'd been hurt and get her tested for drugs and STDs. We'd get her on Depo-Provera, the new birth control shots. I had talked to her about safe sex over a year ago, but had no idea if anything stuck. I needed to call her therapist. She had suggested the possibility that Jenny might need psychiatric care like Robert had, especially if she got so out of control I couldn't keep her safe.

Was that overkill? Was I just defaulting to that option because the county would pay for it?

It was almost 10 p.m. I stood in the BART station, scanning the faces of the riders who disembarked every fifteen minutes. I was surprised there were so many young people out on a weekday evening and struck by how much they looked alike: the boys in saggy pants and grunge plaid and the girls sporting a trashy look, with torn shirts and low-slung jeans exposing their underwear. I noted how annoyed I was by this sloppiness, recalling my own college hippie days. My parents had been disgusted that I didn't shave my legs or wear a bra. How did I become such a fuddy-duddy?

After a half hour, I spotted Jenny riding the escalator down to the street level. Her eyes caught mine, then looked away. She wore a knit cap pulled low over her forehead and a puffy jacket that didn't belong to her. As she headed toward me I saw her jeans were torn at the hem from dragging the ground and remembered the argument we'd had about her ruining her new clothes to achieve this look. She pushed through the turnstile and shuffled over, slump-shouldered and sullen. In my mind, I was grabbing her, shaking her hard, and crying about how she made me sick with worry. She'd love it if I reacted that emotionally: the big payoff. I looked at her, waiting for her to speak, to explain, to apologize. She said nothing. I turned and walked toward the car and she followed me a few steps behind.

35

REPAIR WORK

As I sped through the winding curves skirting the hills near Mt. Diablo, I felt a tug and wobble, and recognized the feel of a blown tire. I eased off the gas and tapped the brake, focused on maintaining control and finding a place to pull over. There was nowhere to call for roadside service, but I wasn't too worried. I'd changed tires many times, and once with this car a few months earlier. I was more concerned about being late. I had promised Jenny I would take her to a concert in the park, the last of the season before the rains started.

Jenny was staying in a therapeutic group home in Pleasant Hill, some thirty miles from Livermore. There she received twenty-four-hour supervision from trained professionals who helped her with daily living skills and schoolwork and kept her off drugs and out of harm's way. A psychiatrist from the local hospital was conducting an assessment of Jenny's mental health issues and providing her with a cocktail of medications to help manage hallucinations, addictions, and depression.

The right front tire hung from the wheel, twisted in a wad. I chocked the good tires with flat stones I found nearby and popped open the trunk. I pushed aside the emergency items to get at the spare and the tools. Ever since the 1989 earthquake, I had stowed old running shoes, a solar blanket, a first aid kit, and a jug of water in case I had to spend the night in the car or hoof it home. The jack, lug wrench, and spare tire were where I'd left them after the previous flat. I laid the solar blanket on the ground, felt under the chassis for the spot to brace the jack, and raised the car enough to loosen the lug bolts. My actions felt automatic, like I'd done this a hundred times. Compared to what I had been through in the past year, a flat tire was a walk in the park.

At the age of fifteen, Jenny was a chronic runaway and an addict. She snuck out at night, skipped school, and disappeared for days at a time. Once, she ran away to Auburn to her birth mother. When Jenny showed up at her doorstep, Lisa Clyde had the good sense to contact the authorities, not wanting to push her luck by harboring another runaway child. I filed missing persons reports with the police three times over a nine-month period. The first time I was shocked to learn the form required me to agree to release her dental records in case they found a body.

After that, the routine of reporting Jenny missing no longer affected me. I reached a place beyond stress, something like numbed resignation. Nothing fazed me. Jenny ran with a rough crowd of older boys, trading sex for the drugs and alcohol she craved. The stew she ingested prompted several emergency room visits. Her therapist and social worker agreed she was spiraling out of control and needed the drastic intervention of the group home. The county had said they would pay for this program just as they had paid for Robert's Edgewood stay. I was desperate for help and needed a break from all the drama and stress.

I stomped on the wrench until the lug nuts loosened, and then jacked up the front end. A late-model Dodge truck pulled in front of my car and a white guy in his mid-thirties hopped out of the cab. "You need help?" he asked.

I stood and pulled the lug wrench from the jack, holding it like a weapon. "I got it," I said. I didn't smile.

His head jerked back as if I'd slapped him. "Okay, then," he said. He climbed into the truck and drove off in a spray of gravel. I shouldn't have been so rude, but I was in no mood to be messed with.

I slid on the spare, fastened the lug nuts, and jacked the car down to the pavement, tightening each lug nut by jumping on the wrench. It was hard to roll the damaged tire so I pushed it until it was positioned in front of the trunk. With a stoop and a shove, the bad tire was in. My hands were filthy but my clothes looked okay. I'd wash up once I got there.

The large group home was located off an exit ramp near a residential neighborhood. It tried to look like a homey place with a lawn and hanging plants, but the parking lot and chain link fence gave it away as the institution it was. A staff member checked me out through a peephole before opening the door. I explained why I was late, showing her my dirty hands. As I was led to the restroom for a wash-up, I saw Jenny in the atrium smoking with a half dozen other girls. She had on a tight, low-cut T-shirt that emphasized the rubber tire around her middle, the weight gain a result of new medication. She pointed me out to the others and doused her cigarette. Her friends glowered through the glass.

"I'm afraid Jenny has something she needs to show you," the assistant director said. The staff there looked almost as young as the residents. "She did this last night with the help of a couple of the others." Jenny took a side glance at her, then looked straight at me and stuck out her tongue. A crude stud was cushioned there, slightly off center.

Jenny watched for my reaction, her face a mix of defiance and fear. What was I going to say? Was I going to yell at her? Was she afraid I didn't care enough to yell at her?

"That looks like it hurts," I said.

"Not too much." She shrugged and glanced over at her friends watching our little drama. I had grown immune to these pleas for attention and kept my face frozen in a tolerant smile.

"Why don't you take that out for the time being," I said. "I don't want you to get an infection."

Her shoulders slumped in disappointment, playing to the audience, but I saw relief wash over her face. I don't know whether she was grateful for my caring or she needed someone to tell her to remove the painful spike.

"Go take that out and then we can go. You want to go to Chevy's for dinner after the concert?"

She nodded. "I need some things from the drug store too," she said.

"Okay. Hurry up or we won't get a good seat."

I watched her walk to the bedroom she shared with two other girls. The smokers in the atrium turned back to their gossiping. The kitchen was busy with staff and girls preparing the evening meal. A TV blasted from an adjacent room, and an argument ensued in one of the back bedrooms. Twenty girls lived there and each had chores and school work and social lives, just like a regular family. My home was empty now—too quiet. Other people were raising my children.

36

What Is Left Behind

The ceiling in my bedroom was painted peach. In fact, all the ceilings and walls in my new townhouse in downtown Pleasanton were painted that color. I had wanted something cheery and warm and feminine. After spending most of my life compromising with others, I picked a color *I* liked. When I told the painters what I wanted, they looked at each other and shrugged. They joked that painting the whole house that color made them sleepy. I learned later that the rosy peach I had selected was close to what was used in prisons to keep inmates calm. On those rare times I brought dates home, I watched them cringe. One said my townhouse felt like a giant womb. That didn't bother me a bit.

The twenty-five-year-old ranch-style house in Livermore had become too much for me to take care of. Every weekend I mowed the lawns front and back, pulled weeds, and made repairs. My commute to the Oakland-based nonprofit I managed required a mind-numbing slog through an hour of traffic twice a day. This newer townhouse was smaller and easier to care for and saved me forty minutes a day in driving. Pleasanton was a charming suburban town with restaurants and a farmer's market, and was only a bus ride away from the BART station. I'd always wanted to live here, and with the equity from the Livermore house, I could finally afford it.

It was perfect for Jenny and me. I had hoped she'd be able to leave the group home soon and come back to live here. On her weekend outings, she had helped me pick out a new carpet and the paint colors. I bought her a new bedroom set with a bedspread to match the curtains. An award-winning high school was a short walk away. I had hoped she'd meet new friends there and leave behind the bad influences at her old high school in Livermore. We planned to have a fresh start—Jenny, me, and the two cats.

But she was gone. I had no idea where she was. Her group home hadn't kept her safe after all. Like Robert's group home, they weren't licensed to restrain chronic runaways, only to impose restrictions or try to talk them out of leaving.

During the first couple of months Jenny lived there she had run off for several hours during what was supposed to be a quick walk to the store. That excursion resulted in lost privileges and extra chores. A few weeks later, she and another girl ran away during the night. The San Francisco police returned them at three in the morning after they and a couple of men tried to enter a sex club together. The hero of that episode was the club bouncer, who spotted the underage girls and called the police.

Jenny had been gone for several weeks now. I lay in bed and stared at the freshly painted ceiling, thinking about all the time I'd spent worrying about her. What was she doing at that moment? Did she have enough to eat? Where was she staying? Lisa Clyde swore she hadn't seen her and, for once, I believed her. I fretted about the hitchhiking she must have done or the sleazebag she probably hooked up with to get a ride to wherever she went. There are costs for those favors and Jenny was accommodating, especially if drugs or alcohol were involved. I checked messages often, hoping she'd at least let me know she was okay. I found myself scanning crowds for her, amazed that so many girls her age looked the same—strawberry blond hair pulled back with a scrunchy, an oversized sweatshirt, and too-long jeans dragging the ground. It was as if an army of scowling, sullen teen girls had been cloned as my daughter to prevent me from finding her.

The group home filed the police report for me, but by now I knew from experience that didn't mean much. The police don't look for runaways; they just check the computer for juveniles who happen to be picked up for a violation. No news meant she was either staying out of trouble or she was dead. I chose to focus on the former.

Over the years, Michael and I had relied on a gallows sense of humor to get us through the tough times of raising these children. While some parents bragged about what colleges their kids were trying for or their stellar GPAs, we set a lower bar. If we could keep Jenny and Robert alive till they reached eighteen, it was an achievement. If either of the children ever got their high school diplomas and went on to college, it would be icing on the cake.

But college was out of the question for Jenny. At sixteen she could barely read or write. The legal drugs she took for depression and to help her sleep kept her so drowsy she nodded off during class, and her illegal drug use had caused other damage, as yet unknown. Her special-ed teachers tried to help her catch up with her credits as long as she was willing to work. During meetings with her teachers, Jenny made promises I knew she wouldn't keep. Beyond her disabilities, addictions, and possible mental illness, Jenny knew how to manipulate people, a survival skill she had learned as a tot.

Maybe those survival skills were helping her now. I could only hope. I convinced myself that maybe she'd talked some nice people into letting her stay with them in exchange for housework or child care. I couldn't bear to think about her on the streets, sleeping under bridges or with strangers for money. Young girls like her were snatched up and lost every day, either killed for a moment's thrill or sucked into a cycle of prostitution and drugs with no way out. This was a parent's worst nightmare: not being able to protect a child from her own bad choices.

I had nightmares about Jenny during this time. I saw her body lying in a ditch covered in dry leaves. I saw her funeral. During the day I was sick with worry and found it hard to concentrate on my work. I got a prescription for Paxil and began seeing a therapist, grieving for my daughter in tear-filled sessions. I tried to focus on the sweet memories I had of the little girl who loved to dress up in my old clothes and pose like a model. Her playfulness and good nature had brought sunshine into my life. When she graduated from eighth grade, she looked so beautiful in her pale yellow summer dress. That day I imagined how she'd look as a grown woman and was so proud of her.

Would I ever see her as a grown woman?

Did Jenny have any idea how painful it was to not know where she was and to worry about her so much? I stared at the peach-colored ceiling and wept until I couldn't breathe. Then I got out of bed and blew my nose and shifted the pillows so I could sleep on the dry one. Finally, I was wrung out and unable to cry anymore. All I could do was pray. Though I no longer went to church, I needed to believe in the power of prayer. That was all I had left.

37

Lock the Door and Throw Away the Key

I remember the exact moment I thought I'd like to kill her, or at least make her very uncomfortable. Getting Jenny to go to school had now become a daily battle. I stared at my daughter buried under her bedcovers, oblivious to her alarm clock and my shouts to get out of bed and get dressed. I could almost see myself filling a bucket with icy cold water and dumping the contents on her head in one scream-inducing pour. I steadied myself by gripping the doorknob to her bedroom and squeezed my eyes shut to erase the fantasized child abuse.

So much for my grand experiment. When I had brought Jenny home from Reno after she disappeared for three months, I told her she didn't have to go back to the group home as long as she followed my strict rules: go to school every day, help with chores, and get a job and stick to it. No drugs or alcohol. No sneaking out or skipping school.

It worked for a while. Jenny returned to high school just in time for her junior prom, so Michael and I sprung for a new outfit, hairdo, and limo rental. She looked so beautiful and sophisticated in the deep blue sheath dress and matching heels. I took dozens of pictures of her and her date, and relished the role of a proud mom. Later in the summer, she and I drove to Ashland, Oregon, vacationing at a bed and breakfast, seeing a few plays, and rafting the Rogue River. It was as if I had gotten my sweet daughter back. Everything seemed fine as long as we didn't dig too deep.

We never talked about what happened during her months away, and we didn't discuss that tension-filled day when I picked her up at Reno juvenile hall and drove her home. She never apologized and I never told her how I felt about her running away. I didn't think she could have tolerated hearing about how much pain I experienced. I was aware of how fragile she was and how tenuous our relationship had become. It was too much to expect her to maintain that level of equilibrium, considering the demons she was battling. But one evening we had it out.

"Do you really think you're fooling me? The school calls my office when you miss class."

Jenny didn't respond, merely sank deeper into the sofa, focusing on petting one of the cats. Her baggy jeans and sweatshirt were torn and stained. Her unwashed hair hung around her gaunt, acne-scarred face in greasy strings, and her teeth were yellowed from smoking and not brushing.

"You promised your teachers you would work during study period to make up for the classes you missed. Don't you want to graduate this spring?"

"I do." She looked up at me, hurt.

"Well, how do you think that's going to happen unless you do the work?"

"I *am* going to graduate—you'll see. But nobody's helping me. I need a better tutor."

"You have a tutor. But you're not showing up for the sessions, and you have to do the homework she gives you. Nobody's going to do it for you."

"I try but she doesn't listen. I don't like her and she hates me."

I really wanted to throttle her. I was so weary of her making excuses and blaming others—and we had other problems.

"Jenny, yesterday I had eighty dollars in my purse and now I only have forty. I would like the money back. I need it for groceries."

"Don't look at me. Maybe you lost it. You're getting forgetful." She smiled as if she'd found a solution to a problem.

My jaw tightened at her sarcasm. "Go clean your room. Then come down and help me with dinner." I was weary of hiding my purse and considering putting a lock on my bedroom door.

She stomped up the stairs and slammed her door.

I believed every parent of a seventeen-year-old had plotted homicide at some point. What made this different was the pent-up resentment I carried for the days and nights lost to emergency room visits, filling out police reports, and worrying about where she was. I was out of ideas and conflicted because I was hoping to start a new chapter of my life.

I was in love with Steve, a sweet man I'd met through an online dating service. After a year of spending time together on alternate weekends while Michael supervised Jenny, we were considering moving in together. Jenny had broken all the house rules I had set as conditions for her living with me, but she needed to be supervised till she turned eighteen. I decided to take Michael up on his offer of switching primary parenting duties, a generous gesture to make up for my bearing the heavy load of caring for Jenny the past few years.

Michael lived nearby, in a townhouse in Pleasanton he'd bought to be closer to his work and to help out with Jenny. Since our divorce, we had been getting along well. I knew I could rely on him to keep an eye on Jenny if I had a business trip or needed to work late. Our new plan was that she'd move in with him for the rest of her senior year and I'd be the weekend parent for a change. I was happy to get my life back and grateful to Michael for being so fair.

The first couple of months of the new arrangement went smoothly, with Jenny following his rules—like she'd followed mine in the beginning. But it all fell apart when she found a new boyfriend, a high school freshman with his own behavior problems. They skipped school and went off drinking and smoking pot together. I was pretty sure they were responsible for vandalizing the front of my home, pelting the garage door with eggs. Michael said she snuck out at night and was often missing in the morning when he needed to take her to school.

Despite our vigilance with her birth control, Jenny became pregnant. I made arrangements to take her to a local clinic. Though she was nearly eighteen, the father was only fifteen, so the options were limited. Considering the age difference, we were fortunate her boyfriend's parents didn't press charges.

Shortly after her eighteenth birthday, Michael called me at work. "She's been arrested and sent to Santa Rita."

"What happened?"

"She got in a fight at school. She pulled out a jackknife and threatened a girl."

"Oh, dear God, but why is she in Santa Rita?"

"She's eighteen. She's an adult. Jenny's old enough for the women's jail now. Isn't that just great? For good measure, she's been expelled."

It took a moment for this to sink in. I was horrified by the thought of my daughter in jail and devastated that she had been expelled. Everyone had worked so hard to help her catch up on missing credits and graduate with her class.

"What do we do now?" I asked. "Are we supposed to post bail?" I had no clue how that worked, but guessed it must cost a lot.

"I called over to the jail. She's going to be released tomorrow because the school dropped the charges. There's no point spending the money to bail her out if she's getting out anyway. It would do her good to spend the night there. Maybe it'll make an impression."

It would be a relief if something made an impression on Jenny.

The next day Michael picked her up at the jail, then called me later to let me know how their conversation went.

"She says it's the other girl's fault," he said.

"So what else is new?" I said.

"She said the other girl disrespected her boyfriend. She showed her the knife to let her know she meant business but she never pulled it on her."

"Let me guess. She's the victim, right?"

"You got it. We talked about the fact that since she's expelled she has to get a job. I can't have her lying around the house all day."

"Let's see how that goes. She hasn't been able to keep one for more than a couple of months."

In the weeks that followed, Jenny filled out job applications but made little effort to follow up. She became more aggressive with Michael, screaming at him when he asked her to help keep the house clean. When she threw a vase at him, we began to suspect meth use. Five foot four, she weighed less than a hundred pounds, and her face bore scarring more severe than typical teenage acne. She didn't seem to sleep or eat, and Michael rarely saw her except when she came with a carload of friends to retrieve a change of clothes. Money and other items went missing from his home. He agonized over what to do.

"Catherine, I can't live like this. I never know what I'll find when I come home. Sometimes her friends are there, and they scare me. I can't keep anything of value in the house. It's gotten so I'm afraid to come home. I feel like I have no choice."

"You've done everything you can. I've done everything I can. If she won't abide by your rules, you have to put her out. Let her be on her own for a while. Then maybe she'll get a job or go back to school or both."

Michael gave her a month's notice to find another place to live. On the deadline, he helped her carry her things to a friend's car, waved good-bye, and changed the locks.

We continued to help her as best we could while keeping our distance so she would know she was on her own. She found a room to rent with a friend in exchange for providing child care and worked part time at a pancake house. Michael bought her a used car to get her to and from work. I kept in contact with her by phone and an occasional meal out. We met up one afternoon at a sushi restaurant in Pleasanton.

"You look like you've lost some weight," I said.

She picked at her bento box, shifting the tempura from one side to the other. "Yeah, I can fit into a size zero. Can you believe it?"

"Aren't you hungry?"

"I am."

"You're not really eating."

"I'll get a to-go box. I shouldn't have eaten before I came here."

"How's your job going?"

"Okay, I guess. But there's one girl there I can't stand. She's stuck up and tells me what to do. She's dating the boss and she thinks she can get away with it."

"That's not good. Are you getting along with your housemate?"

"I think I'm going to move."

"Why?"

"She says she wants someone else who will pay more rent for the room. It's not fair."

"What are you going to do?"

"I don't know." She stared off into space as if there were ideas on the light fixtures. The table wobbled from her nervous foot jiggling.

"You know, Jenny, I worry about you. You look like someone who's taking meth. You know how dangerous that is, don't you?"

She sat back and shook her head in denial. "What makes you say that?"

I touched my cheek and then pointed at her acne scars. There were other signs: weight loss, lack of appetite, and paranoia. With a job she had more money in her pocket and more money to spend on drugs. She mumbled something about going to the drugstore and asked the waitress for a takeout box. She had friends to meet in Fremont and had to get going.

I walked a thin line with Jenny. If I confronted her, she shut me out. If I lectured her, we didn't speak for weeks. I didn't want to push her away, so I decided I wouldn't confront her any further. I knew I couldn't prevent her from taking drugs. I just hoped I, or someone else who cared for her, would be there when she hit bottom and needed help.

A few months later, I learned she was pregnant and planning to wed in Reno.

38

Last Chance

She's gone."

"What do you mean?"

"Yesterday, while I was at work, she left the kids with Rosa and said she was going to a party. No one's seen her since." Rafael's voice muffled as he spoke to one of his two boys, my grandchildren. The other wailed in the background.

I switched the phone to the other ear and reached for a pen and paper. "I'm over a hundred miles away, Rafael."

"I know." Rafael choked as he tried to speak. His accent was heavy, and it was hard to hear him over the children. "How could she do this? She knows I have to work, and I'll lose my job if I don't show up." Except for food stamps and a bit of welfare, Rafael's job as a cook was the primary income for Jenny and their two boys, Nicolas and Michael.

"She isn't picking up her cell phone?"

"I've left messages and it goes straight to voice mail."

"Does Rosa have any ideas?"

"No. And she's mad she got tricked into keeping the boys last night. *Hijo, I'm on the phone.* I've warned Jenny that if she did this again, I'd take the boys to live with my mother in Mexico."

"Rafael, we've talked about this. You can't take the boys across the border without both parents' permission. Let's solve one problem at a time. I'll call Michael and see if he can watch them today while you're at work and I'll drive back later. Did you call her other friends? What

171

about filing a missing-persons report?" I was furious she would leave her husband and two toddler sons like this. It had to be drugs.

"She's been hanging out with new people I don't know. Could you file the police report?" Of course, I should have thought of that. Rafael needed to avoid interactions with the police. Eight years in this country and he'd never had a reason to come in contact with the authorities. He'd lived a charmed life, until he married my daughter.

I hung up the phone and called Michael.

"You've got to be kidding," he said. "She did this a couple of months ago, left Rafael stranded with no ride home from work. That time she came back the next day." I hadn't been aware of this earlier episode. Michael and I found we had to keep each other informed to know what was really going on with Jenny's family.

"I was going out with friends tonight, but I can cancel." Michael said. "I'll take the boys today, but I can't tomorrow. I'm teaching a class. When are you driving back from Mendocino?"

"This afternoon. They can stay with us tomorrow, but let's hope she's back by then. I saw her last week and she looked so thin. I think she's back on drugs."

"That would explain it."

I updated Steve on the situation, and we began closing up the house, a vacation getaway we'd purchased last year. Steve and I now lived together in my townhome in Pleasanton. My daughter's late-night emergencies and last-minute needs often disrupted our plans. He was understanding, but not happy with how my daughter upset me. I wiped down the counters and emptied the dishwasher while Steve packed the car. While I worried about how I was going to entertain two toddlers for an indefinite time, Steve drove us home and tried to cheer me up.

"It'll be fun. Just pretend you're camping with the kids," he said.

"Easy for you to say—you're going off to work tomorrow morning." I was self-employed again and worked at home. I would have to rearrange my schedule for the next day so I could shop for kid food and file a missing persons report.

The next day, after confirming that no one had heard from Jenny, I went to the police. Though my best guess was she was partying with friends, it didn't hurt to have them looking for her. There was always the chance she had been assaulted or kidnapped, and I would've felt terrible if we hadn't taken the precaution.

I was childproofing the house, throwing blankets over my glass tables and securing cupboard doors, when Michael showed up with the two boys and their overnight bags, car seats, and diapers. Nicolas, just turned three, was cranky from being shuffled from house to house. Little Michael, at fifteen months, toddled off in pursuit of our new kitten.

"The boys were really good—you just have to keep your eyes on them all the time. Nicolas runs off if you don't have a hold of his hand when you're out walking."

"Okay, thanks for the warning." Fifty-eight now, I was no spring chicken, so these two were going to be a handful.

I pulled out every toy from the downstairs closet and laid them on the living room floor. We stacked blocks, banged on the xylophone, and rolled wooden balls across the floor until Nicolas started throwing them. The cat hid under our bed out of reach. When Steve came home from work, the boys piled in his lap and they watched *SpongeBob Squarepants* on Nickelodeon. After a bubble bath, teeth brushing, and a story, the boys fell asleep on the air mattress we laid out in our bedroom. They stayed with us for two nights, till one of Rafael's friends said his wife could babysit until Rafael got off work. I made arrangements to pay for the child care so I could get back to work myself.

After four days, the police found Jenny's car in a local motel parking lot. She and another woman were arrested for drug possession and booked into Santa Rita jail. Because of our previous experience with Jenny in jail, we knew how it worked and didn't post bail. Michael, Rafael, and I agreed to meet with Jenny at my home after her court appearance the following day. We needed a chance to clear the air with her. I was angry she had abandoned her family and worried I'd lose my temper when I saw her.

It was sunny but cool, a break from the overcast weather of the New Year. The Christmas decorations were boxed up in the dining room waiting till Steve and I had a spare moment to store them in the attic. Michael came early so we could organize our thoughts.

"At this stage of my life, I am not taking care of two toddlers," Michael said. I shared that sentiment. As much as I loved my grandsons, I had a wonderful life with Steve and was worried I'd have to give that up.

"Rafael is threatening to take them to Mexico."

"Let him. His mother has never seen the boys. It'll be good for them."

"I've seen that part of Mexico, Michael. It's pretty dismal. It's moot anyway. Until his status changes, he's limited in what he can do unless Jenny consents."

The doorbell rang. Rafael entered with Jenny in tow.

She avoided my gaze and as they sat down, I saw why. Crusty scabs covered her right cheek. Rafael leaned forward on the sofa and stared at the floor, somber and saddened. I offered them sodas and went to the kitchen to fetch them. When I returned, Michael and Rafael were talking quietly about the boys. Jenny wore a scowl and looked ready for an argument.

"So what did the courts say?" I asked.

Jenny pulled some papers out of her purse and slapped them on the coffee table. "It's all here. Random drug tests and I have to go daily meetings for three weeks and check in with a counselor once a week."

I stared at her. "Why are you the one who gets to be angry here?" I said.

"Everybody is ganging up on me. That's the reason for this meeting, right? I'm sorry, okay? I just had to get away."

"Get away? You abandoned your family. If Michael and I hadn't stepped in, Rafael would have lost his job. What were you thinking?"

Michael interceded, seeing I was close to losing it. "Jenny, everyone was worried about you. Why didn't you at least let us know where you were?"

"I needed a break. It's too much taking care of the kids." Jenny's face contorted in misery. She looked at me for sympathy, but that was a mistake.

"Well, welcome to the real world," I said. The bottled-up resentment for all the pain she'd caused over the years bubbled to the surface. "Welcome to motherhood."

Jenny jumped off the couch and yelled, inches from my face. "I told you I was sorry." She fell back and buried her face in Rafael's arm, sobbing. Jenny had never been this aggressive with me, even in our worst moments. Her exaggerated reaction clued me in to the probability she was experiencing withdrawal.

Jenny's husband looked older than his twenty-seven years. He focused on the floor and quietly spoke his piece. "I don't care if you've been with someone else. We can get past that, but our boys need you. If you leave me again like this, I am taking them away and you'll never see any of us."

"I'll never do this again, I promise, Baby. I'm so sorry."

"You have to do the program the judge says. If you don't you're going back to jail."

"I will, I promise."

I watched Rafael lay down the ground rules, talking through how Jenny would get to her classes now that her driver's license had been revoked. Who would watch the children, and how she would get to her counselor in Hayward.

"I can pay for child care for a few more weeks till you get on your feet," I said.

"I can help on the weekends, while Rafael is at work," Michael said.

"Everyone will help you if you stay on track, but can you tell that everyone is fed up?" I said.

Jenny scooped up the court documents and put them back in her purse.

Our relationship was very complicated now. My priority was making sure my grandchildren were safe. If she couldn't take care of them and she put them at risk with her drug use, I'd call Children's Protective Services in a heartbeat. I'd already contacted them once when their apartment became so filthy it caused the children to be chronically sick. I often found the boys unwashed, in dirty clothes, and playing among piles of garbage and dirty dishes. My attempts to help her clean and organize her household helped the situation for a day or two, but then she was back to her routine of visiting with friends and napping.

As they stood to leave, Jenny looked as if she wanted some reassurance from me that I had forgiven her. I started to offer a hug, but the coldness in her eyes stopped me. Or maybe it was my coldness that stopped her.

I nodded to Rafael and said good-bye to Michael. There was something unspoken among the three of us. We were sharing a load none of us wanted.

39

THIS IS YOUR LIFE

Hi Catherine, this is Robert. Just thought I'd see how you're doing and let you know what's going on with me. I think I'm up for a promotion. Give me a call when you get a chance. My schedule changes every day, but I'll call you back when I can."

Robert and I spoke by phone every few months, and when he called it usually included a request for money. I didn't mind giving him a little here and there. I think that's what most parents do for adult children if they can. I helped out Jenny and her family with rent and groceries, and I saw them often these days because they lived in Livermore nearby, but my connection to Robert seemed more tenuous. I wanted to reconnect with my son and was disappointed he might view me as an ATM. I called him back the next day at a time I thought he'd be in.

"Hey, Robert, what's going on?"

"Oh, hi, just a sec." He held his hand over the receiver while he spoke to someone.

"Okay, sorry about that. Say, thanks for calling me back. I wanted to let you know I think I might get a promotion to manager."

"Great. Are you getting the raise you wanted?"

"Mostly better hours and benefits. The pay raise isn't much."

"Well, that's something."

"Say, I have to get to work in a few minutes, but I was wondering if you could help me out. I'm moving into another apartment and need some help with a deposit."

"I can help a little bit. How much do you need?" Robert had moved in with a girlfriend in nearby Marysville just a few months ago. I wondered what that meant.

"Three hundred would help. I've got the rest. Uh, Sandy and I broke up so I have to move out."

"Sorry to hear that."

"It's okay. We're still friends."

"You know, I worry about you. I hope you're not continuing to support Lisa and Karl. That could wreck your finances." When Robert lived with his grandmother he helped provide for his birth mother and her new young son, Karl.

"I haven't talked to her for a while. Grandpa kicked her out. She and Uncle George weren't getting along."

"I just want you to focus on getting yourself on your feet, maybe take those classes at the community college you were talking about. My offer still stands about helping with tuition, you know."

"If I get this promotion, I'll have set hours. I haven't been able to fit in school with my schedule changing every week and all the overtime."

"Okay. I just think it's a good idea for your future, so you can make more money later. Did you get the cash and the photos I sent you in your birthday card?"

"I did. Sorry I didn't mention it. Thanks for the money. I really didn't have any pictures of me when I was little, so that was great."

"I thought you'd like that one of your eighth birthday party at the miniature golf course. Do you remember when that one kid knocked the golf ball clear out of the park?"

"Vaguely."

"Last time we spoke you said something that made me think you don't remember much of your childhood."

He said nothing at first. Maybe he didn't want to hurt my feelings by bringing up some of the sad times.

"You know, all I remember is Edgewood." This was what I was worried about. Robert had lived with us for more than five years before we had to send him to Edgewood Children's Center. What did he remember of his home life with us?

"Do you recall going camping? Picking out pumpkins? Decorating Easter eggs? What about all that cooking you did?"

More silence then, "I guess it's all a blur."

"What if I sent you more photos. I can pick a few out of the two albums I have. I can get them copied at Walgreens."

"If it isn't too much trouble ... Say, I have to go."

When Robert hung up I felt frustrated, and I knew I'd sounded like I was pushing him into looking at things he didn't want to remember. I wished I could reach through the phone, take ahold of his arms, and look him in the eye. I wanted to convince him how hard I had tried to be a good mother to him. How in spite of a rocky marriage, all the adoption court battles, and the struggles to find him the help he needed, I had done my best. Maybe it would be a while before he could understand that.

I pulled out the thick photo albums I'd kept from the time with the kids, looking for pictures that might recall a good memory. As I thumbed through the albums, I reflected that in snapshots our life looked like any family's—camping, holidays, Scouts. But with us, there was always a backstory.

There were pictures of Robert in his Little League uniform, posing with his team. Three years in a row Robert begged to sign up for Little League, but after a few games he became discouraged and wanted to quit the team. I remembered the tug of war we'd once had getting him to a Little League game.

"Robert, we went over this. Once you make a commitment to be on a team, you can't quit. Your teammates depend on you," I said.

"Nobody likes me. They make fun of me when I go up to bat."

"I'm sure it's not as bad as all that. Go put your uniform on. It's time to go. If you don't show up, your team will have to forfeit."

"I hate that uniform. It's ugly and I hate baseball."

"I understand you've changed your mind and you don't have to sign up next year. For now, you have to see this through, even if you don't want to."

Robert hung his head as he returned to his room to dress. He came out wearing only the uniform shirt over his jeans, so I sent him back to his room to finish dressing. We were late to the game, and his team and coach were waiting. I apologized to the coach and joined the other parents in the stands. When it was his turn at bat, Robert stepped forward into the pitch and was hit. His strategy of getting on base without trying to swing at the ball was routine enough to earn me pitying looks from the other parents. I had no idea if he remembered Little League as a good memory, but I tagged the picture to copy later.

I tagged a few photos of all of us camping, coloring Easter eggs, and opening Christmas presents. He looked so proud, posing with one of his culinary achievements, a tuna casserole. Robert still liked to cook, and it was a point of pride.

I paused at the photo of the wrestling competition. The picture was not very good, since I took it from the stands, but you could see Robert and another boy in the middle of the mat. Robert was being held down by the much larger boy, his head wrapped in a hold. This was when Robert was in eighth grade, shortly after he'd been discharged from Edgewood the first time. He seemed to enjoy the sport, but at his first competition no one in his weight category was available, so he was with a much heavier boy. Regardless of the unfair match, Robert made a valiant effort. Other parents in the stands noticed how hard Robert was trying, and a rally of applause cheered him on. "Look at that kid," someone said. "What heart." What heart, indeed. I was never more proud of Robert than I was that day. Tears clouded my eyes as I tagged that photo. I hoped he remembered that event as a success even though he lost.

I flipped through the album for pictures of our cats, knowing how much Robert loved them. Sammy, our small Cheshire who chattered like a monkey, eventually became ill with congenital heart failure. We could have kept him alive for a while with pills, but Sammy balked at the medicine and ran away. While Robert was home from Edgewood for the weekend we spent much of the time looking for our lost cat, handing out flyers and walking the country roads behind our home calling his name. I was worried he was sick, lying in a field. When I thought I spotted him, Robert climbed a fence to check it out. But the lump in the distance turned out to be a rock, and eventually we returned home to wait. Sammy was found later, but I never forgot how compassionate and thoughtful Robert was during that sad time of looking for our lost, sick cat.

I tagged more than thirty photos for Robert. I wrote dates and identifying captions on the backs of each and mailed them off to him. I'd hoped the photos would trigger memories and we could talk about our life together. Maybe we could clear the air and I could tell him what I went through to adopt him. He could fill me in on the parts of his life I had missed when he was at Edgewood, or at the group home, or when he was living with his birth mother. But none of that happened. He thanked me for sending the photos and said nothing more about them.

40

CHANGING OF THE GUARD

The room was perfect. The bed and breakfast suite near downtown Auburn had a large room that included the kitchen, the dining room, and the living room with a gas fireplace. The spacious bedroom had a king-size bed. It was decorated for the holidays, including a small fake Christmas tree in the corner. I had picked this place because it was just a few blocks from where Jenny and her family lived; they didn't have a car, so they could walk over. Jenny, Rafael, and their three children were now living with her birth father's second wife and her teenage daughter. Robert, his girlfriend Nadia, and their two-month-old, Jacob, were also living in Auburn. We had all planned to meet here to celebrate Christmas together.

The weather turned gray and cold, and a misty rain slicked the streets. Jenny didn't want to walk in the weather, so Steve chauffeured her and her family to the room in shifts. I stayed behind so there'd be space for everyone in our little Toyota. When they returned, seven-year-old Nicolas and five-year-old Mikey dashed past me to explore the room. When they saw the presents I'd piled by the Christmas tree, they each let out a whoop.

"Look at all the presents!" Mikey said. He began searching for the ones with his name.

"Can we please open them now?" Nick asked, running up to me with raised eyes and hands held in prayer.

"No, you have to wait," Jenny said. She shooed him away, giving him a stern look. "Hi, Mom," she said. She wrapped one arm around me and gave me a sideways hug. It had been a couple of months since I'd seen her and she looked sleek and sophisticated in a gray sweater, tights, and a scarf. It had now been four years since the meth binge, and her rosy cheeks and healthy weight were a testament to sobriety. Rafael came in behind her, carrying two-year-old Veronica. She was dressed all in purple, including the boots I'd bought for her birthday. Her thick dark hair was tied up in pony tails and her bangs hung in her almond-shaped eyes. She buried her face in her dad's neck, still shy around me. Rafael had put on a little weight too, but looked happy to be there. He hugged me and nudged his daughter to do the same.

"Give Grandma a kiss, Ronnie," Rafael said. Veronica leaned forward and made a smacking noise that was close enough.

"Boys, stop running," Jenny said.

"They're okay, Hon. We got this place so they could run around and not bother anyone. Better than meeting at a restaurant, don't you think?"

"Nice place, Mom."

"Steve wanted us to be comfortable. We'll order pizza as soon as Robert gets here."

"I got his text. He's on the way," she said.

"Come here, boys, and give me a hug," I said. Both of them rushed me like linebackers, and I folded them together and kissed the tops of their heads. "I miss you guys." It had been four months since Jenny's family had been evicted from their Livermore apartment. Auburn was more than two hours away from Pleasanton, and a weekend visit every other month was all we could manage.

"We miss you too, Grandma. Hey, can we sit on the bed?" Nick asked.

"Sure." I knew they were going to do more than sit. They ran from the room, threw off their shoes, and took a running dive onto the large mattress.

"Thanks for getting them, Dear," I said. Steve had settled onto the sofa, and I squeezed in next to him. "You're a prince." Steve rolled his eyes and patted my hand. He enjoyed hanging out with the boys now that they were older. They called him Grandpa Steve and loved to roughhouse with him.

Rafael saw Robert's large white Chevy truck pull up in front of the room and opened the door. Robert beamed as he entered, carrying his two-month-old son and a diaper bag the size of a suitcase. Nearly thirty now, Robert was muscular and tattooed with close-cropped hair and a trendy day-old beard. Rafael took the bag while Robert brought Jacob to me to hold.

"Do you remember Grandma?" I asked the little bundle. His head wobbled toward me as he heard my voice. He had been five days old when I first saw him at Robert's apartment. That was also the first time I'd met his girlfriend, Nadia, a tall, blond woman with sharp features, several years younger than him.

"Nadia's sorry she can't be here. She had to work," Robert said.

"Oh, that's too bad. Maybe we can come over tomorrow before she goes to work?"

"I think that's okay, but let me check with her."

"What kind of pizza does everyone want?" Steve asked.

"Pepperoni," Mikey said.

"Cheese," Nicolas said.

While we waited for the pizza to arrive, we opened the presents: gift certificates for my children and clothes and toys for the grandkids. For the boys I got a bowling set and a Jenga wood block puzzle as well as books and art supplies. I had to be careful not to buy things that took up a lot of space or made noise; Jenny's family was piled into one bedroom while their stuff was in storage. The situation was supposed to be temporary, but I didn't hold out much hope they could get their own place with all the evictions on their credit report.

Robert held Jacob in his lap while he opened his presents—more toys and clothes. They already had a lot of newborn clothes, so I had gotten him jeans and T-shirts for a six-month-old.

Jenny tried to keep order by handing out the gifts one at a time. She collected the wrapping paper as it was tossed on the floor and deposited it in a large trash bag to keep the floor clear. "I really like your outfit," I said. Jenny beamed. She did look great. I tried to give Jenny compliments when I could. Our interactions were often stressful, involving her asking for money and me expressing frustration over her and Rafael's financial decisions.

Robert gave Jacob to me to hold again, and I fed him a bottle of formula his father had prepared.

"He really eats a lot. He's gained four pounds since he was born," Robert said.

"Are you getting any sleep?" I asked.

"I try to feed him at night when I can. Nadia has to work in the morning, and I don't go into work until later. We're getting into a routine, I think." Robert worked as a farmhand and did construction work on the side while Nadia worked at a local deli. Her mother babysat when there were gaps in the schedule.

"What an adjustment, huh?"

"Yeah, but it's so interesting. He changes every day. He looks around when he hears my voice." On cue, Jacob turned his head toward his daddy, then realized the milk had stopped flowing and started to whimper.

"You have to hold these bottles a certain way," Robert said. He corrected the tilt so the milk flowed better. I smiled at the idea of my son teaching me how to feed an infant.

"Would you hold him for a while, Steve? I want to take some pictures."

Steve started to protest, but I smiled at him with a *Please, do me this favor* look and placed Jacob in the crook of his arm, positioning the bottle at the angle Robert had instructed. Steve was uncomfortable with babies, but I wanted to take his picture with Jacob.

"There. Now smile." I snapped Steve's picture. His smile was photogenic but his eyes said *Don't leave me alone with this baby.* I held up my finger, indicating I would just be a minute, and went around the room taking pictures of Robert and Rafael drinking beer together, Jenny helping Veronica try on one of her new outfits, and the boys setting up the bowling game.

"Oh, Ronnie, time for a change," Jenny said. The boys held their noses so we knew what we were in for. "Baby, would you hand me the diaper bag?" Rafael left the kitchen stool to fetch the bag for her, and Jenny laid a changing pad on the floor and began the cleanup.

"That reminds me—I'd better check on Jacob." Robert stuck his nose next to the baby's bottom as Steve passed Jacob over. "I was wondering about that," Steve said.

"Yeah. You're right," Robert said.

I chuckled at Steve's relief and the timing of the dual diaper changes.

"You know, I thought we'd never get Jenny out of diapers when she was little," I said.

Jenny looked at me, wide eyed. "Mom," she said.

I realized too late I'd embarrassed her. "Sorry."

I sat back on the sofa and watched Jenny and Robert wiping bottoms, unfolding the fresh diapers, and tugging the little outfits back on. They were both patient and gentle and proud of their little ones, smiling at me when they saw me watching. My eyes filled with tears and I placed my hand over my mouth, hoping no one had noticed. Mikey stopped his playing and came to stand next to Steve. "Is Grandma sad?" he asked.

Steve looked at me and smiled. "This is what Grandma looks like when she is very happy," he said.

The Easter Moose

YUMMY BUNNY CAKE

1 PKG. PILLSBURY PLUS WHITE CAKE MIX
1 CAN PILLSBURY READY TO SPREAD VANILLA
   FROSTING SUPREME
14 OZ. BAKERS ANGEL FLAKE COCONUT
   FOOD COLORING
   BAKERS CHOCOLATE CHIPS
   JELLY BEANS
   RED STRING LICORICE

PREPARE AND BAKE CAKE IN 2 CAKE PANS EITHER
8 OR 9 INCH ROUND PANS AS DIRECTED ON PACKAGE.
COOL COMPLETELY. CUT CAKE AS SHOWN IN DIAGRAMS
FROST SIDE OF EACH CAKE. ASSEMBLE PIECES AS SHOWN IN
DIAGRAMS ON A COOKIE SHET, LARGE TRAY OR 18x15
INCH CARDBOARD COVERED WITH ALUMINUM FOIL. FROST
TOP OF CAKE. SPRINKLE ABOUT 2 2/3 CUPS COCONUT
EVENLY OVER YOP AND SIDES OF CAKE, GENTLY
PRESSING COCONUT EVENLY OVER TOP AND SIDES. TINT
COCONUT: IN A SMALL BOWL TOSS 3/4 CUP COCONUT WITH
2 to 3 DROPS RED FOOD COLORING UNTIL EVEN COLORED.
REPEAT WITH 1 1/4 CUPS COCONUT AND 2 to 3 DROPS
GREEN FOOD COLORING. SPRINKLE PINK COCONUT OVER
THE EARS AND BOW TIE; OUTLINE WITH CHOCOLATE
CHIPS. DECORATE BUNNY FACE AS SHOWN IN PICTURE.
SPRINKLE GREEN COCONUT EVENLY AROUND CAKE.

FOUND IN A MAGAZINE·MOM

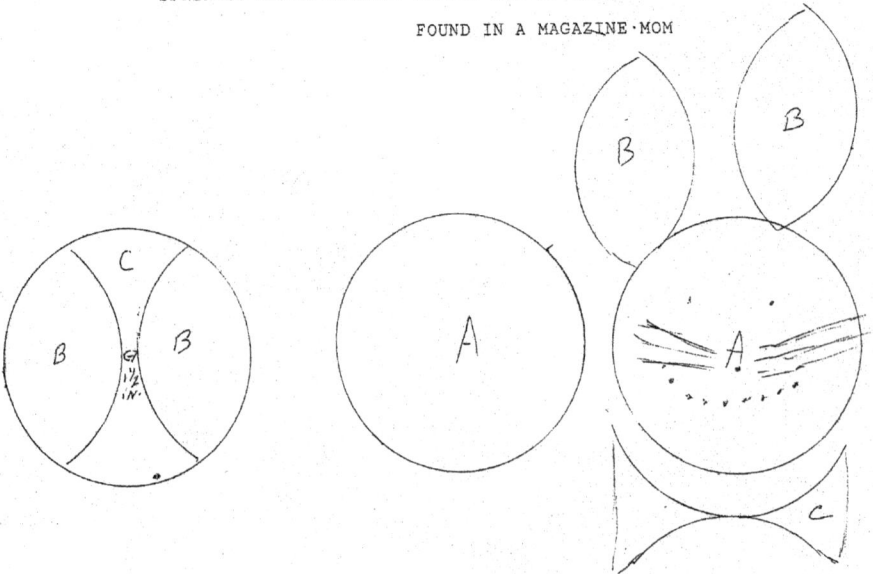

Foster Adoption Resources and Advocacy Groups

Dave Thomas Foundation for Adoption: Resources, facts, and connections for parents considering foster adoption. https://www.davethomasfoundation.org.

Adopt US Kids: A federally funded site that provides a directory of children available for adoption as well as resources for prospective parents. http://adoptuskids.org.

Fostering Families Today Magazine: Helpful hints, articles on topical issues, advocacy update, and book reviews. http://www.fosteringfamiliestoday.com.

Foster Focus Magazine: The go-to source of foster care news and information for anyone involved with the foster care industry. https://www.fosterfocusmag.com.

Adoptive Families Magazine: Success stories, issues of interest to adopting parents, help column, and resources. https://www.adoptivefamilies.com.

Adoption Learning Partners: Videos and training materials to prepare prospective parents for adoption. http://www.adoptionlearningpartners.org.

CASA for Children: These volunteer Casa Appointed Special Advocates are appointed by judges to work in the court system on behalf of abused or neglected children. http://www.casaforchildren.org.

About the Author

Catherine Marshall's stories about parenting and other real life adventures have been featured in several anthologies and magazines including the *Noyo River Review*, *Foster Families Today*, and *Tales of Our Lives*. She resides in the San Francisco Bay Area and Mendocino, where she has a consulting practice specializing in helping nonprofits and community groups effect social change. She is the author of *Field Building: Your Blueprint for Creating an Effective and Powerful Social Movement*. Her website is www.catmarshall.net.